Every Day Jesus

Experience the Jesus Who Ignites Your Soul

By Dave Holland

Daily Jesus Series

Copyright Information

Every Day Jesus

DEDICATION

To Jesus Christ who loved me enough to save me
from myself. To my wife, Jonie, who daily gives me
love and joy with the reminder to love God and
people with my whole heart. To our children –
Jessica, Lisa, Mindee, Justin, Skyler, and Sheldon,
who show me that miracles happen every day
through the people we call family.

ACKNOWLEDGMENTS

I thankfully acknowledge the contributions of the
following people: *Everyday Jesus* is a better book
because Jonie gives me constant encouragement.
Many thanks to Job Vigil and the North Platte
Telegraph, who opened the opportunity to write
about the Lord in a weekly column. I'm grateful to
Wanda Brackett, who taught me so much about
writing, and to Linda Lacey, who did the heavy
lifting in editing this manuscript. Bill Brown, Don
Yoxsimer, Larry Fowler and Kathy Stiles helped
clarify the flow of thought and logic in many of the
chapters. I am in debt to each of these wonderful
people.

You can learn more about Dave and his books by going to Daveholland.org. By joining the email list there you will also benefit from his blog and free postings.

Table of Contents

Day 1

Words That Swell

As a sixteen-year-old new believer in 1970, I was expected to go to the new youth group Bible study on Friday night. Our church leadership was oblivious to the real world and didn't realize that anybody who mattered went to high school football games every Friday night.

My high school team was undefeated and scheduled to play the highest-ranked team in Los Angeles the night our youth Bible study was to begin. I struggled with my sense of priorities and fortunately, I decided to put Jesus first and went to the Bible study. Revving up my *Honda 90* motor scooter I braved the autumn evening air to ride five miles to the home Bible study.

Arriving late to the meeting, I discovered there were no seats left. So I plopped on the floor next to the door. Our host was a single, middle-aged woman named Melba. Her place seemed overly warm and for the first time I got a good look at her. She had graying hair and very thick eyeglasses. I recognized her from our church as she played trombone in the church orchestra. Melba worked as an operator for the Ma-Bell Telephone Company back when live operators had to connect callers to their party. There just wasn't anything about Melba that was cool – all the cool people were at the game anyway.

She got the Bible study underway with some over-the-top enthusiasm as I was starting to fade into slumber. I drifted back into consciousness to hear Melba say, *turn to Romans 12*. Somebody bumped my elbow and handed me a New Testament. As I fumbled with the pages I'm thinking, "Matthew...Mark...Luke...Romans 12. Yep, found it!" At that moment a God-thing happened.

As I looked at the words on the Bible page they swelled to about five inches tall, and the letters pulsated with life. *Now, THAT is cool! How does she do that?*

The Word of God grew before my eyes because a pure-hearted saint shared her life with me - a self-absorbed and egotistical teenager and changed me forever. It was as if God were shouting at me through a bullhorn.

I pray *Every Day Jesus* will minister to you in the same way. I owe it to *Melba the Trombone Player.* May Jesus cause the words of Luke's Gospel to grow in your eyes and breathe courage into your heart.

Luke's Gospel is the Word of God for us – authoritative and unalterable truth. I have cobbled together Church history with ancient legends to recover Luke's perspective. Sit down with Luke and a cup of coffee and watch Jesus draw near.

Picture Luke as a young Greek slave raised by a prosperous landowner named Theophilus, living in first-century Syria. Seeing the potential of this young man, the benevolent master pays for Luke's medical education and would later grant him his freedom. Presumably converted by Paul, Dr. Luke travels extensively and records the events of the great Apostle Paul's ministry. That journey eventually leads him to Israel and the roots of his new faith. Luke gathers first-hand evidence and embraces the real Jesus. The journey comes full circle when he delivers his divinely inspired manuscript to his old friend and benefactor, Theophilus.

EVERY DAY JESUS

As I write the words of this book I picture you and pray God will enlarge your vision of Christ. I wish we could sit down in comfortable chairs at *Starbucks*, drink coffee and share our thoughts along this amazing trip. Let's revisit together the life and times of Jesus of Nazareth, King of all the nations of the earth. May God use Luke's Gospel and this book to stir great change in us – a change that alters us into the likeness of Christ. Romans 12:2, NIrV, says,

Don't live the way this world lives. Let your way of thinking be completely changed (altered, transformed). Then you will be able to test what God wants for you. And you will agree that what he wants is right. His plan is good and pleasing and perfect.

Pray with me:

Jesus, I'm not sure what lies ahead but I know I want You with me. Make Your Word large in my eyes. I don't want to just read Luke - I want to experience You in the drumbeat of my life. May these next forty days make me strong in my faith in You while growing my love for others. Thank you for Luke taking me by the hand and leading along the pathways of Your life.

DAVE HOLLAND

Day 2

Luke is Just Like Us

Our dear friend Luke, the doctor,
and Demas send greetings.
Colossians 4:14

Jesus alters and guides the course of my life like God directs the rivers and the seas. It's not always pleasant but it seems to flow. He slowly shapes and forms my character – he's been at it for over forty-five years. I'm an old dog. I've howled at many moons and pissed on a few fire hydrants. Thankfully, Jesus has persevered through my mistakes, and altered my life's trajectory in ways only He could have mapped. God never gives up on us.

Everyday Jesus describes the life work of another disciple of the Lord – Luke. Of all the Bible writers this disciple is most like you and me – a Gentile, who never had the opportunity to meet the tangible, living, breathing Jesus. The big bang of Christ's life - the resurrection - exploded on the scene long before Luke became a Christian. Like Luke, we share that lack of first-hand experience.

Luke's search for the real Jesus drove him to retrace Christ's steps and moved him to interview first-hand witnesses. His attention to historic detail surfaces throughout the book. As a medical doctor, Luke gives educated observations the other gospel writers neglected. Luke's personality teamed up with the Holy Spirit to drive him to dig like an archeologist. With painstaking patience, Luke brushes away the inaccuracies, myth, and half-truths to write an amazingly accurate account of who Jesus really was as he walked the earth. This sacred journey changed Luke's life in unimaginable ways and his writing bursts with energy to encourage us.

The Holy Spirit inspires Luke to serve as our guide. Unlike the other inspired authors of the Bible, Luke is not writing for Jewish interrogators – he is writing for the Gentile Theophilus and to the Gentile readers beyond – people with a mindset formed by Western Culture. People like you and me.

Every day people are encouraged to engage in this devotional - I'm picturing the contractor in his truck at lunchtime, the professional at his desk, the homebodies in their recliners; the woman on her coffee break. Each section takes about fifteen minutes to read. Perhaps you read in quiet morning moments, or the late-night hours before going to bed – whatever time works for you - do that.

Pray with me that Jesus bends the course of our lives toward His destiny for us. Pray that we eat spiritual food as we read this devotional. Partake of the meat of the Gospel with the flavor of a contemporary story mixed with beefy chunks of prayer power. Pray for the same burst of energy and encouragement that sustained Luke as he uncovers the love of Christ for the Gentile world.

Important Instructions

1. Don't skip reading the scripture! Begin each chapter of *Everyday Jesus* starting with the next sequential passage in Luke, though there is occasionally some overlap.

2. Pray the prayer! Say them, speak them out loud and believe God hears them. Let Jesus' Presence loose in your space.

This whole exercise should take less than 15 minutes. Engage your mind, challenge your heart, and bring your soul to the table – let the Word grow in your eyes. Pray with me now.

Dear Lord Jesus, I come to ask that You change me into Your likeness. I ask that You help me become a faithful disciple who loves You and glorifies Your Name. May the Holy Spirit use this simple devotional and the Gospel of Luke to guide my steps into Your pathways. In Your Name, I pray, Amen.

DAVE HOLLAND

Day 3

Investigating Reality, Part 1

Many have undertaken to draw up an account of the things that have been fulfilled among us, just as they were handed down to us by those who from the first were eyewitnesses and servants of the word. With this in mind, since I myself have carefully investigated everything from the beginning, I too decided to write an orderly account for you, most excellent Theophilus, so that you may know the certainty of the things you have been taught.
Luke 1:1-4

What is the one thing you need for salvation? Certainly, you need the blood of Christ to atone for your sin, and yes, it's essential to receive God's grace. But, without the *revelation* of these blessings we are lost, utterly lost.

Luke investigates for us the revelation of salvation. Sound and solid, it is anchored in the historical reality of the life of Jesus. Immovable truth that saves us from ourselves oozes out of every pore of this gospel.

We live in uncertain times. People change careers, spouses, churches and homes multiple times. Pope Benedict comments in a homily in 2005; *We are moving toward a dictatorship of relativism which does not recognize anything as for certain and which has as its highest goal one's own ego and one's own desires.*

I don't want to live a life ruled by my ego or the whims of my appetites. I want to build my life on something that is sound and sure, even when the world around me is a ball of confusion.

Dr. Luke lived in times like ours. He wrote his gospel for people like us. The other authors of the scriptures were Jewish with a common sense of history and values. In contrast, Luke was a Gentile with a Greco-Roman worldview writing to a culture without knowledge of the true God. Reared without any sense of biblical values, Luke comes to the knowledge of God by his conversion to faith in Christ.

Luke researched the facts of Christ's life with an unquenchable appetite for the essential truths of His life. He wrote for his Greek friend Theophilus, and for us, a clear narrative of Christ's message imparting a *certain* faith. The Gospel of Luke stills our stormy vacillations with a *sure* word and a multitude of facts.

Verse one details the purpose of Luke's gospel. In my words this verse says, *the things fulfilled, accomplished and completed; or, those things that are most surely believed among us.* He is expressing a belief in Christ that is the same as Peter, John, Paul and the early believers. I hunger for that conviction and Luke serves it to us warm and tasty with the aroma of authenticity.

The early church universally accepted Luke's gospel as true. Verse two confirms that Luke spoke to eyewitnesses of the events recorded. He wrote this narrative and circulated it among people whose very lives verified their authenticity – the people who were there did not challenge Luke's account, they affirmed it. What we have today is an accurate revelation of Jesus on which to build our faith.

Luke describes the *servants of the word* as those people who passed the knowledge of Christ's life to him. He was not an eyewitness himself, but he researched Christ's life among first-hand witnesses. That same word speaks to us now. Luke concludes this section by defining the central purpose of his gospel - so *we might know the certainty of those things in which we have been taught.*

Peter amplifies Luke's message in II Peter 1:19-21, *And so we have the prophetic word confirmed, which you do well to heed as a light that shines in a dark place, until the day dawns and the morning star rises in your hearts; knowing this first, that no prophecy of Scripture is of any private interpretation, for prophecy never came by the will of man, but holy men of God spoke as they were moved by the Holy Spirit.* (NKJV).

I remember a story about a young professional musician who visited his high school music teacher and asked, *So, what's new?*

The teacher responded by banging his tuning fork on the desk and a resounding 'A' note rang out. *Do you hear that? That's an 'A'. Upstairs is a soprano who rehearses endlessly, and she is off-key. Next door is a cello player who does not play well, and there is an out-of-tune piano on the other side of me. Terrible noise surrounds me.*

Plunking the 'A' again, he continued, *do you hear that? That's an 'A', yesterday that was an 'A', today that is an 'A' and tomorrow that will be an 'A'. It will never change, it is always beautiful.*

Luke demands this same quality of certainty. Our knowledge of Jesus stands on the immoveable reliability of the Word of God - *Jesus Christ is the same yesterday and today and forever.* Hebrews 13:8, NKJV. Good news that never changes. Want more beauty in your life? Less confusion? Too busy for God? Start building on the sure word of the gospel and commit right now to learn all that God has for you.

Dear Lord, sometimes my life feels like I am living in a tornado — I give you my confusion. Clear my muddled thinking and ground me in Your sure Word. Give me the backbone to stand when I am tempted to compromise my faith in You. Help me to weigh the changes occurring today that lean against your Word. Grant me the inner focus to hear Your Voice above the screaming voices of my culture. I ask that I could know Jesus through my devotions in Luke. Help me to sit quietly with Luke like a live-in roommate and a close confidant. In Christ's Name, I pray, Amen.

Day 4

Investigating Reality, Part 2

Many have undertaken to draw up an account of the things that have been fulfilled among us, just as they were handed down to us by those who from the first were eyewitnesses and servants of the word. Therefore, since I myself have carefully investigated everything from the beginning, it seemed good also to me to write an orderly account for you, most excellent Theophilus, so that you may know the certainty of the things you have been taught.

Luke 1:1-4

Sometimes we feel like the oddball, the outsider, the misfits. We're the last one picked for the team in the playground game or the one nobody wants to sit with at lunch time. The gospel evangelist Luke knows how we feel because the reality is that we are all outsiders. He writes the good news of Jesus to draw us into the family of God.

Luke penned his gospel for Gentiles, formerly outside of the household of faith, now brought near by the blood of Christ. He invites us to become friends of God, and to hang out with the Trinity, do lunch with Jesus – He sees us and embraces us wherever we are.

Eugene Peterson, translator of *The Message* states, *Luke is the most vigorous champion of the outsider. As an outsider himself, the only Gentile in an all-Jewish cast of New Testament writers, he shows how Jesus includes those who are typically treated as outsiders by the religious establishment of the day: women, common laborers (sheepherders), the racially different (the Samaritans), and the poor.*[1]

Luke goes to extraordinary lengths to embrace these folks and encircles everyone in the gospel orbit. The Gospel of Luke is not the only story of Christ's life, as there are other inspired gospels, but *it is an invitation* to non-Jews to join the living, breathing family of God.

Who is this man Luke? He is highly educated and employs the finest Greek language in the New Testament as he engages the linguistic forms used by classical Greek historians. Paul and Luke traveled together as companions in the ministry, and the Apostle christened him *the beloved physician.* Loyalty pulses through Luke's veins as he endured with Paul right up to the Apostle's execution in Rome.

Who is Theophilus? He is mentioned twice in the New Testament. Luke addresses him as *most excellent,* a title usually reserved for kings and Roman dignitaries. His name means *Friend of God* or *God-lover.* Cobbling together the story, I see Theophilus as a wealthy Greek patron to whom Luke shares the story of his Savior.

You must ask, *why did Luke write his gospel rather than simply using existing ones?* As a Gentile in a predominantly Jewish church, I believe he wanted to paint the gospel story with Gentile colors as he saw the salvation message for every kindred, tongue, and tribe.

---

[1] Peterson, Eugene. *The Message, The Bible in Contemporary Language.* NavPress, Colorado Springs, Colorado, 2002: page 1846

As a former servant, Luke also saw the resulting social uplift that Christians could experience. The masses suffered beneath the harsh dictates of the Roman government. Husbands treated their wives like possessions who had no legal standing. Roman masters oppressed their slaves. Luke wrote his gospel to encourage these downtrodden folks.

Luke-the-Gentile didn't get invited to sit with the Jewish believers at lunchtime due to their dietary laws, but he didn't turn inward dwelling on his lack of acceptance. Instead, he turned outward toward those who did not know Jesus, thereby catching us in the gospel net. This record of Christ's life recruits you to become an ambassador who embraces the outsider.

The Apostle Paul agrees in Ephesians 2:9 ...*you are no longer foreigners and aliens, but fellow citizens with God's people and members of God's household.* We are accepted and loved dearly.

We must cast our vision toward those who feel like the outsider. Jesus is with us in the foxhole of life inviting others to come into His rest. We are all outsiders until Jesus embraces us and calls us *beloved.* Now, it's our turn to do the same for others.

Dear God, help me to know Jesus intimately as I enter this journey through Luke's Gospel. I grasp the truth of Your Acceptance and Love. I ask that you help me get beyond mere intellectual truth and receive this into my emotions and my heart. I embrace you - I need Your help giving this acceptance to others. Thank you for making me part of Your family. In Your Name, I pray, Amen.

Day 5

Old Zeke and Barren Liz

*In the time of Herod king of Judea there was a priest named
Zechariah, who belonged to the priestly division of Abijah; his wife
Elizabeth was also a descendant of Aaron. Both of them were
upright in the sight of God, observing all the Lord's commandments
and regulations blamelessly. But they had no children, because
Elizabeth was barren; and they were both well along in years.*

*Once when Zechariah's division was on duty and he was serving as
priest before God, he was chosen by lot, according to the custom of
the priesthood, to go into the temple of the Lord and burn incense.
And when the time for the burning of incense came, all the
assembled worshipers were praying outside.*

*Then an angel of the Lord appeared to him, standing at the right
side of the altar of incense.*
Luke 1:5-12

The couple was old and disappointed with their lives. They
lived obedient to their customs yet found themselves in their
twilight years feeling empty, childless, cursed. Who would have
thought that anything significant would happen through them?

Our scripture reading today bleeds with human despair. Luke 1:5-12 spins the tale of the priest Zechariah and his wife Elizabeth who obeyed all the Lord's instructions. They were entering old age without children in a time when being childless was a curse. Depression dribbles off the edges of this story.

We find Zechariah, an elderly Levitical priest, faithfully fulfilling his duty. At this point in history, he was among roughly twenty thousand descendants of Aaron performing priestly functions. The priests were distributed into twenty-four divisions composed of nearly a thousand ministers. Each division would serve two weeks per year in the temple.

The thousands of priests would draw lots annually to determine who would enter the Holy Place to light the sacramental worship incense before the presence of God. The priest chosen would minister one day and would never be eligible to serve again.

This ritual was a once in a lifetime honor, and Zechariah drew the winning number. The Levitical Priesthood had completed this task nobly for over a thousand years without anything unusual happening. This day would be like no other.

As the masses of people pray for him outside, Zechariah approaches the altar of incense in the Holy Place and the bizarre breaks into reality. Gabriel the Archangel startles him and turns his world upside down.

Until this moment Zachariah's life had been defined by two things – faithfulness and barrenness. His life was average, mundane, and probably boring. In God's economy it is the ordinary days where a person's mettle is proven.

EVERY DAY JESUS

What do you do when you are bored or tired? Watch more TV? More Work? An extra hour or two in the office? Many have an affair, pursue entertainments, or settle for less than their dreams.

Suddenly, piercing the thin veil of our reality, another dimension breaks through. An angel arrives, or an answer to prayer is pronounced, or a revelation of God lifts you to another level. Are you ready to be elevated to spiritual places you have never been before?

Jesus still interrupts our lives when we least expect it. God desires to reveal His great glory to us. I remember participating in a destination wedding in the Dominican Republic. It was a warm, breezy day on the beach, and about thirty people were gathered for the proceedings. I am a minister but was not conducting the ceremony; I sat as a guest in this beautiful resort location.

Minutes before the wedding, I was asked if I would pray a blessing over the couple once the ceremony began. I dutifully complied, happy to be of service. The ceremony began, and I was called forward to pray. I reminded the couple that Jesus enjoyed going to weddings because that's who He is. I gestured down the beach, saying, "Imagine if Jesus came walking down this beach to take part in the wedding."

Then I saw Him. Jesus – walking down the beach toward us. He came, He blessed, He participated. When Jesus enters a common ceremony, life begins to flow. Emotions and feelings are quickened. Joy flows like wine.

Jesus is the God of suddenlies, the God who arrives in the most unpredictable ways. Zechariah was unprepared for God's messenger Gabriel. Are you ready for God to do something *suddenly* in your life? Are you prepared to receive a fresh message of divine grace through the Gospel of Luke, or are you too busy doing life? On your last breath, what will be your last words? To hear from God you must first listen, to see you must first look. Your focus is everything, just ask old Zeke.

O Lord, I pray for a new realization of your reality to burst forth into my life. I'm tired of me, and I'm bored with the struggle. You are the new wine, you are the heavenly truth revealing all that God wants to do in my life. Open my eyes today that I can see the angels working on my behalf and hear the promises you have for me. In your name I pray. Amen.

Day 6

Answer the Phone

But the angel said to him: "Do not be afraid, Zechariah; your prayer has been heard. Your wife Elizabeth will bear you a son, and you are to give him the name John. He will be a joy and delight to you, and many will rejoice because of his birth, for he will be great in the sight of the Lord. He is never to take wine or other fermented drink, and he will be filled with the Holy Spirit even from birth. Many of the people of Israel will he bring back to the Lord their God. And he will go on before the Lord, in the spirit and power of Elijah, to turn the hearts of the fathers to their children and the disobedient to the wisdom of the righteous - to make ready a people prepared for the Lord."
Luke 1:13-17

God is preparing us for something more, and He is patiently formulating His plans with great forethought. We will find fulfillment only when we discover His purpose for our lives. God is calling but will we answer the phone? Are we open to the supernatural move of the Holy Spirit breaking into our lives?

John the Baptist had the luxury of knowing why he was born and Luke 1:13-17 reveals that purpose - to lead others to faith in the Messiah. The people had not heard from God in over four hundred years. They needed a *now* word from God plowing their hearts open to receive the seed of life found in Christ. God's intention for John required purity of life, fullness of the Holy Spirit, and power to invite people back to the Lord.

John didn't perform wonders or miracles; he never raised the dead or healed the sick. Yet, Jesus said that no one was greater than John. John prepared the way for Christ by crying out to God's people, *REPENT!* He preached, *turn away from the mundane things that distract you and devote yourself to God.* These words are just as valid today.

Allow me to share what repentance is not. Mourning over your past misdeeds and shameful behaviors are not repentance. God does not want you to crawl to Him as a worm or grovel like a poor, shameless creature. Repentance means, *to change the way you think.* Allow God to affect your mind and redirect your heart toward Him. Jesus came to facilitate that process. Place your trust in Christ and He removes the guilt. Then, live joyfully with the approval that God gave His Son – it's yours now through repentance and faith!

Think of repentance this way - God is on the telephone calling you, and the prophet in our passage pleads, *pick up the phone and listen to the Lord!* God desires a conversation that brings us closer to Him. The result of that turning away becomes real and visible as we reconcile with our Creator and return to His ways.

Good gardeners know that to produce a harvest, you must first prepare the earth, break open the fallow ground, fertilize the soil and sow good seed. No preparation, no sowing, no harvest. The same is true for us. Good things happen when we turn toward the Lord and let God rototill our hearts and sow fresh grace. The Holy Spirit would saturate our soul like spring rain.

Allow God to speak into your life through the voice of His Word and let the Holy Spirit direct your attention back to Him – is there anything more important than that? I think not. I remember Jack Hayford singing, *Let us search and try our ways and turn again to the Lord, lift our hearts with our hands unto God in the heavens and return again to the Lord.*[2] This song demonstrates the spirit of repentance put to melody.

When I became a Christian at age sixteen, I thought I was the first confessing Christian in our family. I discovered the backstory while I was in Bible College. During my mother's pregnancy with me, she had been an active Christian. A great gulf of antagonism separated my Mom and Dad at that time, and the doctor told my mother that if she didn't improve her emotional state, she could lose the baby she was carrying.

My mother desperately called upon the Lord praying, *Lord, if you spare this child, I will dedicate him to You and name him David.* After my birth, my parents eventually divorced. In the years following their breakup, my mother slowly drifted away from God. Despite her shortcomings, the Lord was faithful in answering her prayer. God later claimed me for Himself.

I answered God's call because of the prayer that had gone before me. John the Baptist followed the prophetic call because of the prayer and events that occurred before he was even born. God is reaching out to you through the events of your life as well – God

[2] Hayford, Jack M. *Sing Praises, A Collection of Songs and Hymns for Today's Church on the Way.* Van Nuys, California, 1976: page 36.

wove His grace into the fabric of your history. Ask God to give you eyes to see His mercy working in your life.

The Lord yearns for us not only to respond to His invitation but also to pray others into the kingdom of God. Christ Jesus the Lord is calling your name right now! Will you pick up the phone and answer Him? Will you also pray for others to answer their phone when God calls? The joy of life resides in living beyond ourselves and dedicating our lives to God's purpose.

My King and My God, make Your plans
and purposes known to me as You did to the
prophet, John the Baptist. I want to serve You as
faithfully as He did. I would be Your Voice
speaking Your Word in the wilderness of this world.
Cross-examine my heart, purify my motives and
sharpen my focus I pray. I must be an open ear
listening to Your Voice – help me to hear Your call
and answer the phone. In Jesus' Name, I pray,
Amen.

Day 7

Shut Up and Listen

But the angel said to him: "Do not be afraid, Zechariah; your prayer has been heard. Your wife Elizabeth will bear you a son, and you are to give him the name John. He will be a joy and delight to you, and many will rejoice because of his birth, for he will be great in the sight of the Lord. He is never to take wine or other fermented drink, and he will be filled with the Holy Spirit even from birth. Many of the people of Israel will he bring back to the Lord their God. And he will go on before the Lord, in the spirit and power of Elijah, to turn the hearts of the fathers to their children and the disobedient to the wisdom of the righteous — to make ready a people prepared for the Lord."

Zechariah asked the angel, "How can I be sure of this? I am an old man and my wife is well along in years."

The angel answered, "I am Gabriel. I stand in the presence of God, and I have been sent to speak to you and to tell you this good news. And now you will be silent and not able to speak until the day this happens, because you did not believe my words, which will come true at their proper time."

Luke 1:13-20

Have you ever been rattled by God? Shocked at His goodness? Amazed that He still loves you despite the things you've done? I have and I'm not ashamed to admit it. I've discovered that God never gives up, He always wins and always has the last word. Denial does not work very well when you are dealing with the everlasting God – especially one who shows up at the most unexpected times.

The Angel Gabriel appears in verse 13 pronouncing ...*do not be afraid, Zechariah; your prayer has been heard. Your wife, Elizabeth, will bear you a son, and you are to give him the name John.* YOUR PRAYER HAS BEEN HEARD!

The elderly priest reacts badly as doubt dribbles out of his mouth in verse 18, *How can I be sure of this? I am an old man, and my wife is well along in years.* To say old Zeke was *startled and gripped with fear* may be an understatement. Zechariah gets caught unaware, unprepared, and faithless…much like most of us.

The angel strikes Zechariah speechless – a minister's worst nightmare. Zechariah walks out from the temple to what should have been the zenith of his career - multitudes gathering to hear him announce the Aaronic blessing. He was supposed to say, *The Lord bless you and keep you; the Lord make his face shine upon you and be gracious to you; the Lord turn His face toward you and give you peace.*

But Zechariah could not speak because of his unbelief. Instead of rejoicing, the silence hangs in the air like a foreboding fog. The people did not grasp the spiritual magnitude of what had happened inside the temple, and the priest was not able to tell them. No faith, no blessing, equals no understanding.

All is not lost, however, as God works in the old couple. Fruitfulness replaces barrenness slowly, silently, steadily. Miraculously, as the baby swells in the woman, old Zeke and Liz turned toward God. Did they deserve such a gift of grace? Certainly not – people never do. Yet God still works.

All the while the words, *Prepare the way of the Lord,* grows quietly in the heart of the prophet living in Elizabeth's womb. The call to repentance that would mark John the Baptist life was born out of the pure, shocking grace shown to his parents. The child would bring actual meaning to their lives, a purpose to live for, and excitement to their casual circumstances.

Many would argue that the Puritan preacher, Jonathan Edwards, was a minister of fire and brimstone. I read his sermon, "Sinners in the Hands of An Angry God," in my American Literature class in high school and was scared spitless. The only clouds in that picture were the clouds of God's wrath hanging over humanity to execute judgment at any moment. The irony was that it was the revelation of God's goodness that motivated Edward's ministry. He saw God as holding terrible judgment back - that people might turn and believe in God's mercy.

The same can be said of John the Baptist. The little boy grew up in a home where his father's failure to believe were evident and overcome. The fire that burned in John's bones was nurtured in a home where grace abounded – the kind of grace that comes to people who have stumbled yet persevered in their lives long enough to see that God never fails in his gracious work. Pray with me that we will be ready for the revelation of God's goodness. You never know when an Angel might show up.

My God, may I be ready for your surprises. May I believe in your goodness even when my heart condemns me as doubting, fearful and unprepared. Your mighty power and righteousness scare me — give me the courage to believe that You are for me and not against me. Forgive me for seeking a sign when you are quietly doing Your gracious work. I pray today in Jesus' name. Amen.

Day 8

Waiting and Wondering

Meanwhile, the people were waiting for Zechariah and wondering why he stayed so long in the temple. When he came out, he could not speak to them. They realized he had seen a vision in the temple, for he kept making signs to them but remained unable to speak.

Luke 1:21-23

Too often our lives are marked by silence when we should be shouting the wonders of God. Doubt and his ugly cousin fear render us mute, unable to speak. There are people that you and I know who desperately need to hear about Jesus – they are waiting to meet a genuine believer and silently wondering what God is really like. We stand like Zechariah amazed but doubting, having seen a revelation of God but silent in its wake.

When I was a young man in high school, I sat next to a beautiful cheerleader named Rose in my photography class. I was so nervous around her I could barely remember my name. My youth pastor had been encouraging our youth group to bring our Bibles to school as a witness of our faith. I had mine with me in class on the bottom of a large stack of books when Rose pointed to the Bible and asked, "What's that?"

My tongue swelled in my mouth and I was barely able to blurt out, "The Bible."

"What's it for?" She said. I blithered out some lame answer and was unable to respond to her sincere question. Insecurity and fear rob us of our senses. Zechariah missed a great blessing that day, but God won in the end – Zechariah and Elizabeth still received their heart's desire for a child.

Our scripture today says, *they realized he had seen a vision in the temple, for he kept making signs to them but remained unable to speak.* Can you imagine how he might signal to the crowd what he had seen? It had to be comical, the kind of stuff Charlie Chaplin movies were made of. Have you experienced God in ways that were hard to describe with words? Old Zeke had the challenge of explaining the inexplicable God without words. Oy Vey! (Yiddish for "Oh, my goodness!)

This passage pushes the boundaries of our faith beyond our safety zone, beyond the prison cell where we have lived. Zechariah believed in God but only so far. "God is great out there in the universe but in my life let's be real, I'm not all that," Old Zeke seems to say. The big, anonymous God up in heaven is harmless so don't expect Him to do something in me. That's how we lose the battle of faith. Our expectations and hope are reasonable, harmless, dumb.

If your dreams are achievable then your God is too small. God would have us believe the impossible, unmanageable, and uncontainable. Don't let doubt sideline you. What should have happened that day the Angel visited Ol' Zeke? The priest should have worshipped God in unrestrained wonder at the amazing thing God was doing in his life. He should have left the Holy Place shouting to the crowd, "God is for us! HE has not abandoned us, a prophet is coming to prepare the way of the Messiah. The time is now to worship the Most High and thank Him for His goodness." The crowd would have gone wild with joy - hope would have seized the day.

The larger point of this passage is that doubt renders us powerless to be helpful to other people. We miss opportunities to share God's life and greatness with others. And, we miss the fulfillment of sharing the extraordinary work of God's grace in our lives. Just as in Zechariah's time people are waiting to hear God's blessing. Will we step up and speak in faith? People are wondering and waiting to hear about the Messiah. God longs to breathe fresh grace into your heart so you can live filled with confidence, joy and peace.

Lord save me from my unbelief and fear, don't let them cheat me from sharing Your love. I repent of the sin of inaction – knowing to do good and not doing it – forgive me Lord. I want to stand and shout your truth, to jump up and down like a child with Christmas morning joy. Give me the words Lord and I will speak to the people of your unspeakable grace.

DAVE HOLLAND

Day 9

From Barren to Happy

When his time of service was completed, he returned home. After this his wife Elizabeth became pregnant and for five months remained in seclusion. "The Lord has done this for me," she said. "In these days he has shown his favor and taken away my disgrace among the people."
Luke 1:24-25

Contrast Zechariah's frustrated silence with Elizabeth's exuberant praise. Faith makes all the difference. This passage concludes in verse 25 as Elizabeth shares, *The Lord has done this for me, in these days he has shown his favor and taken away my disgrace among the people.* The grace of God intercepted their search for meaning, bringing great joy. Elizabeth's response of faith aligned with God's intention to form prophetic power in her womb.

Doubt dominated Zechariah's reaction and unbelief oozes from his words to the Angel. Do we also choose to hover in faithlessness - skeptical of the great and precious promises of God? Do we dawdle in the valley of despondency like Christian in *Pilgrim's Progress,* or dwell in the desert of criticism and idleness like the children of Israel? Are we stunned into silence by the gracious work of God? God forbid.

Look at this passage - admire Zechariah's steadfastness to duty. He was great at showing up but he didn't bring faith to expect the grace of God to meet him. God wants to intervene in our lives. We are spiritual beings who should not be surprised by the supernatural. Zechariah was as skeptical, rational and analytical as we are. He serves as a warning - fill your heart with faith and expectation. May we be ready to respond to the miraculous even though it is long in coming.

The Lord exhorts the Prophet Habakkuk 2:2-3, *Write down the revelation and make it plain on tablets so that a herald may run with it. For the revelation awaits an appointed time; it speaks of the end and will not prove false. Though it linger, wait for it; it will certainly come and will not delay.* In my words – delay is not denial. Zechariah and Elizabeth's desire for a child was long in coming but not rejected. They received their heart's desire. Though we may feel unfulfilled now, God's answer is on its way.

Life gives us plenty of opportunities to be negative or resentful. We can choose to live in those thoughts, or we can start each day with a new attitude. Imagine Elizabeth, her old husband leaves to serve in the temple and comes home unable to speak - but very frisky. "What has gotten into you Zeke?" She must have thought. She goes along for the ride and gets pregnant. She knew the time of the Lord's favor had finally come and she got happy. Hooyah God! If I were Zechariah, I probably would have wanted a little of the credit too, but I think he got happy and recognized the Lord's grace upon their lives.

God took away their disgrace, the scripture says. The Greek word in verse 25 translated as grace infers a slur or slight was made against them. When I was a young Christian in high school the Jesus Movement was in full swing in Southern California. Revival fire blew through my East Los Angeles gang-land community. I remember going into my student government class and as I passed two other students, I heard them sneer, "there's another one of those born-agains," and they laughed. My ears burned with embarrassment. One of those students was named "Dicki" and he was the all-conference nose tackle on our football team. He was slight of build, but so tough nobody wanted to mess with him – including me, so I whimpered away in silence.

Twelve years passed and I was standing in line to enter a pastor's conference in Prescott, Arizona. Standing in bone-charring heat I heard someone call, "Hey Dave." I turned and there he was.

"Hi Dicki," I said, clearly astonished.

"Oh Dave, they don't call me Dicki anymore."

"What do they call you now?" I asked.

"Pastor Richard."

You see, God always wins in the end. His grace somehow prevails. Old people sometimes have babies and unlikely people often come to Jesus. God is waiting to do great things in our lives if we will let Him – dare to believe greatly!

Dear Lord Jesus, come to me in my least expected hour. My heart is set to respond to You and obey Your promptings. Give me the patience to believe You will fulfill the desires You have put in my heart. Prepare my heart for Your coming in unexpected ways. Help me to know the joy of living

DAVE HOLLAND

for You. I pray, Come Holy Spirit and fill me with faith, Amen.

Day 10

The Promise That Means Everything

In the sixth month, God sent the angel Gabriel to Nazareth, a town in Galilee, to a virgin pledged to be married to a man named Joseph, a descendant of David. The virgin's name was Mary. The angel went to her and said, "Greetings, you who are highly favored! The Lord is with you."

Mary was greatly troubled at his words and wondered what kind of greeting this might be. But the angel said to her, "Do not be afraid, Mary, you have found favor with God. You will be with child and give birth to a son, and you are to give him the name Jesus. He will be great and will be called the Son of the Most High. The Lord God will give him the throne of his father David, and he will reign over the house of Jacob forever; his kingdom will never end."

Luke 1:26-33

What is the first thing you need for salvation? Repentance? Faith? Perhaps love? Nope. The first thing that God gives you is a promise. Without God's Word, you have nothing to believe in; you have no hope, no knowledge of salvation.

The Old Testament believers looked forward to the fulfillment of God's reign on earth through the Messiah. Faith in that promise saved them. Abraham was dead in his body but

41

believed against all hope that God's promise would give him children, and God accounted it to him as righteousness. *By faith he dwelt in the land of promise as in a foreign country, dwelling in tents with Isaac and Jacob, the heirs with him of the same promise; for he waited for the city which has foundations, whose builder and maker is God.* Hebrews11:9-10, NKJV.

Mary received a more incredible promise, *You will be with child and give birth to a son, and you are to give him the name Jesus. He will be great and will be called the Son of the Most High. The Lord God will give him the throne of his father David, and he will reign over the house of Jacob forever; his kingdom will never end.* Luke 1:31-33.

No one in history had ever received such a challenge as this. Mary's faith rose up to receive the promise and believed. Imagine if Moses or Elijah had received this Word from God? Moses split the Red Sea, and Elijah raised the dead but, trust me, those men would have run screaming in terror if they thought they had to birth a baby. Mary's response was simply for clarification, *How will this be, Mary asked the angel, since I am a virgin?* Luke 1:34.

The angelic messenger's response was even more implausible, *And the angel answered and said to her, "The Holy Spirit will come upon you, and the power of the Highest will overshadow you; therefore, also, that Holy One who is to be born will be called the Son of God... For with God nothing will be impossible."* Luke 1:35-37, NKJV. The impossible becomes possible when the Holy Spirit comes upon you.

The simple beauty of Mary's next response demonstrates faith in its purest form, *Then Mary said, "Behold the maidservant of the Lord! Let it be to me according to your word."* Luke 1:38, NKJV.

OK, Mary seems to say, *no big whoop, I accept this never before seen on earth miracle, I say 'Yes and Amen God'.* We could take lessons from her faith. What would you say to the Lord in that case? Contrast Mary's response in Luke 1 where Zechariah was given the promise of a son and He didn't believe it. I want faith like Mary's that will rise up and believe the promises of God with humility

Christ fulfilled over three hundred messianic prophecies, including thirty-six specific to His birth. Humanly speaking this is an impossibility. But spiritually this is the completion of God's promise to humanity. Jesus is the promise of God in the flesh – with us – for us – in us.

Over seven hundred years before Jesus was born, the prophet Isaiah says, *Therefore the Lord himself shall give you a sign: Behold, a virgin shall conceive, and bear a son, and shall call his name Immanuel.* Isaiah 7:14, KJV. Mary was a teenage girl, yet she trusted God's promise. The angel proclaimed that she, a virgin having never known a man intimately, could birth *Immanuel – the Son of the Creator of the Universe* - the fulfillment of God's promise to His people. Amazing faith!

Believe the Word of God, believe in the promise of the Savior, and focus your faith on Christ. Mary did it, so can you!

Dear God, help me to lay hold of Your promises today. I am setting my heart toward You believing that You want to do something wonderful in my life. Give me faith to apprehend Your promises. In Christ's Name, I pray, Amen

DAVE HOLLAND

Day 11

The God-Formed Life

"How will this be," Mary asked the angel, "since I am a virgin?"

The angel answered, "The Holy Spirit will come upon you, and the power of the Most High will overshadow you. So the holy one to be born will be called the Son of God. Even Elizabeth your relative is going to have a child in her old age, and she who was said to be barren is in her sixth month. For nothing is impossible with God."

"I am the Lord's servant," Mary answered. "May it be to me as you have said." Then the angel left her.
Luke 1:34-38

My child-like interpretation of Luke 1:31 goes something like this, *Surprise! Mary, there's a baby in your belly.* This simple promise to Mary holds tremendous provision for us. The birth of Christ is beyond eloquent words, so the Angel of the Lord just says it like it is. God is forming in you. Jesus is the ultimate God-formed life.

Clearly, Mary's conception of the Savior was unique to the human experience as she was *overshadowed* by the Holy Spirit. God's explanation of the whole matter to Joseph in Matthew 1:20 pronounces, *that which is conceived in her is of the Holy Spirit.* In my words, the Holy Spirit breathed on Mary imparting to her the genesis of spiritual life, His life, a God quality of life that can be passed on to others.

The psalmist of Israel, King David, drew on prophetic insight when he penned Psalm 139:13-14, NKJV, *For You formed my inward parts; You covered me in my mother's womb. I will praise You, for I am fearfully and wonderfully made.* David knew that it was God at work in his mother's womb, knitting the strands of his life together. David knew he was formed in God's image. God involves Himself directly in David's formation, and He participates in our development as well.

Our problem is that sin pollutes us right down to our DNA matter. Our faults and failures wound us and leave us lying face down in a spiritual ditch. The life God formed in us through our parents is now stained. Unseemly passions compounded by the influence of a corrupt culture moved by unrestrained earthly drives leave us in a raunchy pit.

We fill our lives with lust for more money, power, and sex; well, more of anything that makes ME feel good.

Paul speaks to our dilemma, *I beseech you therefore, brethren, by the mercies of God, that you present your bodies a living sacrifice, holy, acceptable to God, which is your reasonable service. And do not be conformed to this world, but be transformed by the renewing of your mind, that you may prove what is that good and acceptable and perfect will of God.* Romans 12:1-2, NKJV. Don't allow the corrupting elements of the world into your mind and life.

EVERY DAY JESUS

The same God-power that formed Christ in Mary's womb now desires to shapes you and me through the realities of our lives. Difficulties intended to move us toward God work like a carpenter's sandpaper to smooth our rough edges. Victories point us Godward in praise – every time we turn worship toward God we are further shaped into Christ's likeness.

The middle years of my life are marked with the scars of divorce and false accusations. I was emotionally devasted and financially wrecked. As I sat in front of my computer preparing to submit job applications I thought, "I'm not married now I can go anywhere I want on the computer." Porn, gambling, and raunchy websites abound on the internet. The temptation was intense.

But the Holy Spirit spoke quietly to my heart, "What will you become?" It was a pivotal moment for me. I could choose to be perverted by succumbing to temptation or I could yield to the gentle prompting of God and let Him mold me into a man of God. The Lord was focused on my long term benefit rather than my short term desire.

Christ was formed in the womb and lived a holy life filled with the presence and power of God. He did not succumb to the temptations of the world – He overcame them. His sinless life becomes the key to our freedom from sin. When you put your faith in Jesus, God forms a new creation in you – His intention all along.

Through the redemption found in Jesus, we are now free to choose to grow in love, in grace, and His Word. Let God's Word and Spirit shape your life into a demonstration of His grace and glory – allow God's Spirit to form fresh life in you.

Dear God My Maker, I praise You for the miracle of Christ's incarnation as the God-Man. I thank You that He provided the perfect sacrifice for me. Now I pray that You would form in me a Christ-likeness. Make me sensitive to Your Spirit as He separates me from the world. Subdue my sin nature and do Your work of re-creation in me. Do this for Your glory, Amen.

Day 12

When Hearts Leap

At that time Mary got ready and hurried to a town in the hill country of Judea, where she entered Zechariah's home and greeted Elizabeth. When Elizabeth heard Mary's greeting, the baby leaped in her womb, and Elizabeth was filled with the Holy Spirit. In a loud voice she exclaimed: "Blessed are you among women, and blessed is the child you will bear! But why am I so favored, that the mother of my Lord should come to me? As soon as the sound of your greeting reached my ears, the baby in my womb leaped for joy. Blessed is she who has believed that what the Lord has said to her will be accomplished!"
Luke 1:39-45

Baby John must have been an active little guy, kicking and squirming in the womb. But this day is special - Jesus came to his house. John the Baptist and Jesus, each in their mother's womb, met for the first time, and according to Elizabeth in Luke 1:44, NKJV, John *leaped in my womb for joy.* Even before he was born John shows us how to react to Jesus Christ.

Baby John's response to the Lord was powerful, but also instinctive and aware. The fetus in the womb reacted to another fetus in the womb. Thank God abortion was neither permissible nor acceptable in their culture.

It has been over forty years since the Supreme Court decision known as "Roe vs. Wade", and we should grieve the loss of over fifty million aborted children. Pause to consider the lost joys, dead dreams and canceled giftedness that could have blessed humanity through those children. How many prophets, pastors or priests are in that sea of earthly dead? How many Einsteins or Lincolns or Michelangelos are in that vast group? How many women have suffered from guilt and condemnation due to abortion?

Both Elizabeth and Mary became pregnant at the most inconvenient time. Elizabeth was elderly and about to deliver a child that would put her life at risk. Mary was an unmarried teenager who surely suffered social condemnation. Both women saw the miraculous hand of God at work in their lives and their wombs. As a man, I can only observe the miracle of childbirth as an outsider. I envy those women even as I thank God I don't have to go through such pain and responsibility.

Mary's reply to the announcement of her and Elizabeth's pregnancies was, *Let it be to me according to your word.* Luke 1:38, NKJV.

Elizabeth responded to the news of Mary's seemingly illegitimate pregnancy, *Blessed are you among women, and blessed is the child you will bear!* Luke 1:42. These women react with great faith in very unusual circumstances. Would we do the same? There is never a problem greater than God's ability to handle – our challenge is to refocus on the challenge from God's perspective.

This story begs the question, *is there ever an illegitimate pregnancy?* Certainly, it is best when a husband and wife conceive a child. But to consider a child illegitimate because of the parents' circumstances is to deny the miracle of life that has occurred.

Consider this, sunrises occur each morning, and some are gloriously colorful while others are cloudy and dull. The reality is still that the sun still comes up and warms the land. An unwanted pregnancy is a glorious reality to be embraced whether it comes through cloudy circumstances or not.

Mary and Elizabeth encouraged each other with affirming words. To be a Christian is to believe in the God of the impossible and to belong to a family who is there when you need them most. We have the power to encourage and bless each other as Mary and Elizabeth did. Our attitudes and words can make a huge difference in the lives of people facing an unexpected pregnancy; we must choose to affirm life at every opportunity.

I believe the stance of Christian folks should change from *No, no, no to abortion* - to *Yes, yes, yes to life.* Our hearts should leap in the presence of every baby made in the image of God. Christ died for each of us and He lives to lead us to eternal life. Should we not also live to give that hope to others - born and unborn?

Lord Jesus, give me a sensitive spirit like
John the Baptist who leaped for joy in Your
Presence. Give me that prophetic edge that proclaims
Your kingdom and establishes Your reign on earth.
I pray that unborn children in our country would
live and not die. I ask for the boldness of John the
Baptist. In the Name of the Father, Amen

DAVE HOLLAND

The Song of Reversals

And Mary said:
"My soul glorifies the Lord and my spirit rejoices in God my
Savior, for he has been mindful of the humble state of his servant.
From now on all generations will call me blessed, for the
Mighty One has done great things for me - holy is his name.
His mercy extends to those who fear him, from generation to
generation.
He has performed mighty deeds with his arm;
he has scattered those who are proud in their inmost thoughts.
He has brought down rulers from their thrones but has lifted up the
humble.
He has filled the hungry with good things but has sent the rich away
empty.
He has helped his servant Israel, remembering to be merciful to
Abraham and his descendants forever, even as he said to our
fathers."

Mary stayed with Elizabeth for about three months
and then returned home.
Luke 1:46-56

How does a simple, uneducated teenage girl write a song of unparalleled beauty? How do we live a meaningful life of devotion to God in an age preoccupied with politics, sex, drugs and the celebrity cult? People are obsessed with the person they see in the mirror. How do we elevate our lives out of the muck and mire to spiritual significance? The answers to these questions are found in Mary's modest refrain.

Upon learning from the Angel Gabriel that she would miraculously give birth to the Son of the Most High God, Mary erupts in praise toward God in Luke 1:46-55. Widely known as *The Magnificat*, the song takes us by the hand and guides us along the pathway of ultimate Christian praise. Mary focuses on the glory of God. A loose translation of verses 46-47 could sound like this, *My soul is determined to see the largeness of God's work in me – HE is so great! My heart is so happy with my Savior, who has saved me from so much evil.* It's a tune you can sing.

Only Luke's Gospel includes this song as Luke celebrates the underdog - the poor, the non-Jew and women. Luke portrays Mary, not as a victim but as the singer of reversals. She interprets the events occurring in her life through the song of faith. Mary is a person of low regard by most people around her, yet she is lifted by a mighty God. The contrast could hardly be more profound.

The *Magnificat* graphically displays many characteristic features of Hebrew poetry. For example, note the three contrasting parallels in verses 50-53. The proud are upended by the Lord while those who fear Him are exalted. The mighty are humbled while those of low degree are dignified, and the rich are sent away empty even as the hungry eat their fill.

The internal conflicts that must have existed in Mary are astounding. This young, unmarried girl is from a lowly village of a subjugated province in the mightiest empire in the ancient world. Told by an Angel she will be impregnated by the Holy Spirit - the prophetic pronouncement humbles Mary, yet she *believes* this incredible event will occur. Only extraordinary faith could make such a leap. Imagine if you were Mary – would you believe or call a therapist?

Mary meek and mild is really Mary mighty in faith. She sees in this child the reversal of destiny for her life, her nation, and all humanity. She is not a trapped, unwed victim of a condescending, judgmental culture; rather, she emerges as the prophet-poet-participant of the most extraordinary event in human history.

A perplexing question emerges; *how does one remain humble when you are the mother of the Son of God?* Mary is abundantly clear that her humility does not rest on seeing herself as small. Her meekness nestles into the largeness of God. Mary does not grovel in fake humility, but her song instead amplifies the immensity of the Lord in her life and ours. Her faith was shameless and fearless – it lifts my faith to new levels propelling me forward no matter what the obstacle.

Dear God, I give You the trials and challenges that I am facing. I believe You are in the process of reversing my problems and causing me to be an overcomer through Christ. My life is in Your Hands O Lord, and I trust You to lift me above the difficulties that cross my path each day. In Jesus' Name, I pray, Amen.

DAVE HOLLAND

Day 14

Out of the Silence

When it was time for Elizabeth to have her baby, she gave birth to a son. Her neighbors and relatives heard that the Lord had shown her great mercy, and they shared her joy.

On the eighth day they came to circumcise the child, and they were going to name him after his father Zechariah, but his mother spoke up and said, "No! He is to be called John."

They said to her, "There is no one among your relatives who has that name."

Then they made signs to his father, to find out what he would like to name the child. He asked for a writing tablet, and to everyone's astonishment he wrote, "His name is John." Immediately his mouth was opened and his tongue was loosed, and he began to speak, praising God. The neighbors were all filled with awe, and throughout the hill country of Judea people were talking about all these things. Everyone who heard this wondered about it, asking, "What then is this child going to be?" For the Lord's hand was with him.

Luke 1:57-66

The most profound changes often come during the quiet times of our lives. A breakthrough in one's life often follows a long season of boring routine. Hard work on the same tedious job suddenly opens doors to a new opportunity. These demonstrate surprising results following silent periods. The priest Zechariah experienced both a reflective silence and a sudden release that would have a tremendous impact.

Zechariah had received an angelic visitation promising a son, John the Baptist. When the old priest doubted the message, he was struck dumb; not empty-headed, but lacking the ability to speak. Therefore, he could not perform the honorable function of blessing the people at the Jewish feast. Zechariah's tongue was bound for nine months as the angel's prophecy comes to pass in his wife, Elizabeth. That long period of silence was the pivotal experience in Zeke's life.

Faced with a long period of inescapable introspection Zechariah could have descended into self-pity and despair. Inside his head he might have tormented himself with questions, *Why do bad things always happen to me? I blew it; God is punishing me.* Instead, Zechariah stored the treasure of thankfulness as daily he observed his wife's maturing pregnancy.

Zechariah pondered the great thing God was doing for at least nine months. What fills your thoughts in the still moments of your life? What feelings fill your mind? What is the self-talk going on in your head? Do you see opportunities or problems? The choices you make not only dictate your destiny, but they also make your journey either bitter or joyful.

Obedient to the angel's directive, Zechariah wrote the name of his son John and God's healing power suddenly surged – God loosed his tongue. Obedience to God's promises makes all the difference. John's birth was an astonishing surprise that generated thanksgiving in the community, and Zechariah's healing resulted in unrestrained praise.

Out of Zechariah's silence his tongue was released to speak God's words *...and you, child, will be called the prophet of the Highest; For you will go before the face of the Lord to prepare His ways, to give knowledge of salvation to His people.* Luke 1:76-77, NKJV. Not only would Zechariah miraculously speak but, after four hundred years of prophetic silence, his son John would become God's Voice to the world.

John would grow in the silence of the desert emerging as the prophet who would bridge the Old Testament era to the arrival of the Messiah. Something about waiting on God produces the ring of authority in a person's words. Do people listen to your words? More time in silence before God will produce the tone in your voice that people need to hear.

Out of the Judean desert silence comes the dawning of the Dayspring. *Through the tender mercy of our God, with which the Dayspring from on high has visited us; To give light to those who sit in darkness and the shadow of death, to guide our feet into the way of peace.* Luke 1:78-79, NKJV. Luke brings us to the central issue of Zechariah's life and of ours - the sunrise of the light of Christ. Every trial we face, every burden we carry, every boring moment of silence is to bring us to this beginning - the dawning of the Dayspring named Jesus Christ.

Could it be that God will speak to you if you give Him some quiet time? Out of your silence a new person, full of grace and truth, can be born. People will marvel at what God can do with you if you fill your silent times with the wisdom of God. The good news is that you can be born again with the same joy and promise that attended the birth of John the Baptist.

Andrew Murray said, *All the difficulties which are brought forward, as keeping us back from full salvation, have their cause in this one thing: the defective knowledge and practice of waiting on God.* Our business - working and playing – rob us of quiet time with the Lord. If we stop and slow down God will speak. It is out of these silent, waiting periods that God speaks His Word to us, just ask old Zeke.

Holy Spirit, teach me to wait on God, to sit alone in stillness allowing God to speak to my heart. I need Your Word spoken into my mind and soul. Put my heart on trial – sway my heart to reserve the throne of my heart for you. When my time to speak comes, give me the strength to speak what You have put in my heart. Help me find the time to be silent before You. In Your Name, I pray, Amen.

Day 15

Charging Bull

*His (John the Baptist) father Zechariah was filled with the
Holy Spirit and prophesied:*

*"Praise be to the Lord, the God of Israel, because he has
come and has redeemed his people. He has raised up a horn of
salvation for us in the house of his servant David (as he said
through his holy prophets of long ago), salvation from our enemies
and from the hand of all who hate us - to show mercy to our fathers
and to remember his holy covenant, the oath he swore to our father
Abraham: to rescue us from the hand of our enemies, and to enable
us to serve him without fear in holiness and righteousness before him
all our days. And you, my child, will be called a prophet of the
Most High; for you will go on before the Lord to prepare the way
for him, to give his people the knowledge of salvation through the
forgiveness of their sins, because of the tender mercy of our God, by
which the rising sun will come to us from heaven to shine on those
living in darkness and in the shadow of death,
to guide our feet into the path of peace."*

*And the child grew and became strong in spirit; and he lived
in the desert until he appeared publicly to Israel.*

Luke 1:67-80

The bull paws the ground gathering his great strength. He snorts hot breath, rhythmically swinging his horns back and forth slashing the air preparing to mount a charge of brute force. He is both beautiful and dangerous as he strikes terror into your heart. Such is the power Zechariah attributes to the "horns" of Messiah in Luke 1:67-80.

The priest Zechariah watches the birth of his son, John the Baptist, born to him in old age. God frees his tongue and a melody of thanksgiving arises. In that moment of sheer ecstasy, he utters a song of unparalleled beauty using two Old Testament metaphors that live deep in the marrow of his bones. His son has the mandate to declare the arrival of the awaited Messiah.

The first metaphor refers to five references in the Psalms that describe the Messiah as *the horn of salvation.* Zechariah picks up the ancient refrain to announce the coming King. The *horn* speaks of Christ's power to protect us from our enemies, to impart mercy from God and to dispel fear. The Creator of the Universe powerfully frees us from the demons of darkness - worry, lust and anger - to serve God in grace, righteousness and holiness.

For centuries, people have walked in a misguided fear of God. Guilt, condemnation and erroneous notions of God render people numb to His grace. *Christ-the-Bull bursts through those barriers,* to lead us to victory over fear – no matter how large or trivial. He fights for us – not against us, mighty to save and deliver!

Zechariah draws from a second metaphor by calling the Messiah the *Rising Sun,* (NIV), or *Dayspring,* (NKJV). *The rising sun will come to us from heaven to shine on those living in darkness and the shadow of death, to guide our feet into the path of peace,* Luke 1:78. The word

EVERY DAY JESUS

Luke uses is the Greek term *anatello,* translated *rising sun,* meaning *to arise.* Christ is the One through whom light and love come streaming into the world saying to us, *arise from the darkness of sin, hatred, and selfishness.* The Messiah is the Rising Sun, or hope-giver, and His name is Jesus.

Many people feel like the world conspires against them to inconvenience them. Americans are stressed, emotionally drained, and so driven to gain the facade of worldly success that every delay in their day increases their frustration. Rather than living, most people sense they are dying a little more each day. We need the *Rising Sun* to surge upward in our hearts blazing the glory of God.

Dayspring Jesus gives us hope that energizes us. Rather than running on empty, Christ fuels us with positive energy giving us motivation and zest for life. If we dare open our hearts to heaven's hope it will breed optimistic thoughts and the confidence that God is ordering our steps. Before you die, dear friend, choose to really live – dare to live greatly. Believe and experience God in real-time.

Motivational writer and speaker Ken Blanchard will often begin his speeches with an exercise. He asks the audience to get up and greet those seated around them as if they were insignificant. After many dull, awkward moments he interrupts them by changing the request. He asks them to now greet people as if they were their long-lost friends or relatives. The energy and vitality in the room immediately elevates with enthusiasm as people smile, laugh, and hug total strangers. What changed? Their expectations changed with their hope of a positive response.

Close your eyes and talk to God with new expectations - as though you are talking to the King of Kings, Creator, and Sustainer of the Universe. He has control of your every breath. See God like

Zechariah came to see God – with the power of a charging bull and the beauty of the rising sun.

The strength of John the Baptist's ministry lies in stirring God's people with an expectation of the Messiah's arrival. *Charging Bull Jesus* wants to burst into our lives setting us free from the habits and poor choices that have kept us bound. What burst of new courage does the Lord want to pour in your life today? When we receive that revelation, uncontainable worship will overflow our hearts.

When Zechariah received the miracle of a newborn son in he sang God's praises. God can still do something wonderful in your life if you invite the *Dayspring* Jesus to arise and shine. You were born to reflect the sunlight of Dayspring even as the moon reflects the light of the sun. Let your praises and good deeds shine.

Dear Lord – You are the horn and power of my salvation – set me free today. You are the Rising Sun of my life - arise in my heart today with healing in Your wings. I sit before You in awe of your great power but I'm also drawn to Your beautiful majesty. I acknowledge that I need You to free me from the thoughts that bring me down – the fear, worry, and anxiety that plagues me. I choose to be confident, whole and well as I put my trust in You. Be strong in my life today, I pray in Jesus' Name, Amen.

Day 16

Eighty Long Miles, Part 1

In those days Caesar Augustus issued a decree that a census should be taken of the entire Roman world. (This was the first census that took place while Quirinius was governor of Syria.) And everyone went to his own town to register.

So Joseph also went up from the town of Nazareth in Galilee to Judea, to Bethlehem the town of David, because he belonged to the house and line of David. He went there to register with Mary, who was pledged to be married to him and was expecting a child.
Luke 2:1-5

The walk from the village of Nazareth to Bethlehem is over eighty grueling miles. Nazareth sits in the southern range of hills near Mt. Tabor in Northern Palestine. About 10 miles outside the village the land begins to sink into a steep gorge, descending 1000 feet down into the rocky plains of Esdraelon. This would drain a Navy Seal and for a very pregnant Mary it would be grueling – all to birth the Son of God.

Emperor Caesar Augustus issued an imperial order requiring a census of every man in the empire. Joseph was forced to make the trip from Nazareth to his ancestral home in Bethlehem. Mary was not required to register for the census as the Romans only counted men.

What were Joseph and Mary thinking when they set out on this rugged trip together? What would cause Joseph to take Mary along when she was so obviously pregnant? Perhaps Mary's unplanned pregnancy had stirred some uncomfortable controversy in Nazareth?

Imagine the gossip erupting in their small village whenever people saw pregnant Mary - the humiliating whispers and the shaming comments they made about her. Staying alone in Nazareth would be worse than going to Bethlehem as, according to the law, the penalty for this kind of pregnancy was death by stoning. Joseph would have to protect her and shield the baby.

God is unveiling a larger plan for this young couple. Joseph and Mary began the long journey to fulfill the ancient prophecy of Micah 5:2, *But you, Bethlehem, in the land of Judah, are by no means least among the rulers of Judah; for out of you will come a ruler who will be the shepherd of my people Israel.*

Day One: About an eighteen-mile walk from Nazareth would have been a good first day of travel. Set up camp, eat some bread and rest for the next day's journey through Samaria. I imagine as Joseph and Mary lay their heads down that night, they would have wondered, *What lesson is God trying to teach us? What purpose does this trip have for our future? WHY is all this happening NOW God?*

Day Two: They would not likely make it all the way to Samaria on their second day. The road was treacherous with many places along the pathway for thieves to take advantage of travelers.

They would have to make haste and move quickly through this dangerous land. The burden for Mary must have been unbearable, and there was little that Joseph could do to alleviate her suffering. Mary would burst at any moment; only their faith drove them on.

When we are facing dreadful circumstances, such as riding on the back of a donkey or sleeping on the ground, God never lets our trial go to waste. He uses every worry and every hurt to power our resolve. He turns our weakness into motivation as He forms our character. The bitter moments of our struggle cause us to call upon His Name, transforming our faith into endurance.

By the end of day two, they were midway to Bethlehem with forty miles to go. This point in the journey would have been a testing time for Joseph and Mary. Giving up and turning back is most tempting at this juncture. Many of us are midway in our journey with the Lord. God will help you overcome obstacles that block the road ahead of you. There will be days and nights you think there is no way you are going to make it through the gauntlet of trials you face; but you must endure, believe and trust.

There will be problems that make you think there is no way you can make it. Pain, sickness, death, divorce, financial crisis and are ultimately spiritual battles. The vultures are circling overhead – don't blink – keep focused on God's future – the Father walks with you. The good news is you are halfway home. You are not half defeated - you are halfway to victory!

Lord, give me faith in my journey today.
Help me see Your hand in the events of my life –
both good and bad. Fill me with courage to conquer
the obstacles in my path and live beyond my hunger

for comfort. I trust that You are in control and leading me to victory. I can live boldly and fearlessly with You by my side. With confidence in Christ's Name, I pray. Amen.

Day 17

Eighty Long Miles, Part 2

In those days Caesar Augustus issued a decree that a census should be taken of the entire Roman world. (This was the first census that took place while Quirinius was governor of Syria.) And everyone went to his own town to register.

So Joseph also went up from the town of Nazareth in Galilee to Judea, to Bethlehem the town of David, because he belonged to the house and line of David. He went there to register with Mary, who was pledged to be married to him and was expecting a child. Luke 2:1-5, NLT

Sometimes it is so hard to see God's hand working behind the difficult circumstances of our lives.

Halfway to anywhere is the worst part of a road trip. Too far gone to turn back and the destination still seems an eternity away. We pick up Joseph and Mary's journey to Jerusalem after two rugged days of travel by foot and donkey. How did they feel after two days of walking and still a couple of days walk to their destination? How do you feel about where you are in your journey with Christ?

Day 3: Mary is approaching delivery, and the couple is still a long, long walk from Jerusalem. Their tired, aching bodies are screaming at them, *STOP!* The Bible does not say that Mary rode a donkey. We assume they have an animal to carry their food, utensils, and personal things.

If Mary did have a donkey to ride, I could imagine her saying, *Joseph can't you make this thing go any faster?* Just when Joseph thinks they are making good progress, Mary says those familiar words of travel, *I need a potty break.* Mary is human and very pregnant. They probably did not make it as far on their third day as they had the prior days.

Somewhere along the southern side of the Jordan River, before it flows into the Dead Sea, the Holy Family would have stopped near the Jericho area to make camp. As Joseph and Mary lay their heads down that night, I wonder about where their thoughts went? They passed near the Jordan River where their forefather had miraculously crossed centuries before. They were also close to the place where God swept Elijah up in a whirlwind and a fiery chariot. Surely their minds drifted to these historic landmarks that surrounded them. God prepared history to welcome the weary couple and give them encouragement. God has a map for your life as well.

Day Four: Still they are about twenty miles from Bethlehem. Even if Mary had a donkey to ride on, a woman nine months pregnant would not have made it without God's help. There were no rest stops, restaurants or hotels. They would have slept on the hard ground through cold nights and made do with the food they carried. They arrived weary in Jerusalem on the fourth day - God's day.

It was not a Christmas card moment for Joseph and Mary entering Bethlehem. They were physically exhausted, emotionally depleted and frantic for lodging. The poor, weary travelers arrived with only strips of cloth called swaddle to wrap their baby.

Life for them, and for us, is filled with winding roads, deep valleys and treacherous mountains. We all pass over dangerous highways and fearful places. We may think ourselves to be tough, but we need to trust God to make it like Mary and Joseph.

Joseph and Mary had a host of angels watching over them – so do you. There were probably times you would not have made it if God had not been watching over you, protecting you, guiding you, and giving you strength. Thank God for His kindness today. He loves you so much.

Too many times we think we can make it without God's help. Self-sufficiency is our enemy. But if we trust Him steadfastly, He will make a way. We must fight the impulse to run away and instead run through the storm trusting God for victory. We must be willing to make the trip to see what Jesus will do. Are you willing to endure the difficulties on the road that you walk to achieve His destiny for you? At the appointed time God will birth new possibilities in you.

Dear Lord, I feel weary in the journey –
give me the strength to endure and the tenacity
necessary to possess all that You have for me. Help
me see the signs of Your presence along the way.
Bring to my mind the scriptures that will guide me
and illumine my path. I ask you to birth something

new and wonderful through me. I pray this in Jesus'
Name, Amen.

Day 18

The Day Heaven Went Silent

And while they were there, the time came for
her baby to be born. She gave birth to her first child,
a son. She wrapped him snugly in strips of cloth and
laid him in a manger, because there was no room for
them in the village inn.
Luke 2:6

I saw Him, the Ancient of Days, in a vision - The Captain of Angel Armies, the Glory of Heavenly Splendor, the Object of the Father's affections. The Son was resplendent, Light of Light, very God of very God, clothed with power, might and dominion. Innumerable legions of angelic creatures sang his praises and marched at His command. Suddenly, without warning, the Son stood from His throne and strode toward the exit gates of heaven.

The Son descended from His throne flinging off his mantle of omnipotence – the Angel Multitudes gasped. Then He marched toward the gates discharging His infinite knowledge. Finally, draining his omnipresence, He opened the gates to leave. Jesus abandoned heaven's glory to be born a vulnerable babe. For the first time in eternity, heaven was empty of the presence of the Son of God.

"Whoosh! What was that?" the angels cried as the Son of God left heaven and poured Himself into a tiny human body far away in the dark planet. Did the music suddenly stop? Were the heavenly hosts perplexed when the object of their eternal affection was absent? When the Glorious One departed did heaven go silent?

Heaven rejoiced in the radiance of God's glory for eon upon eon. The love dance transpiring between the Father, the Son, and the Holy Spirit twirled in rhythm from time immortal. The friction from their constant expression of love toward one another created such a warm glow that the universe basked in its light. But now, the Son was gone.

How did God feel the day Jesus left heaven to pour Himself into a human body? Visualize the moment the Trinity's love party stopped. Did God grow lonely for His Son? Did He mourn His loss? Did the Father long for the fellowship they had? Did God suffer the empty nest syndrome?

Yes, God knew the end of the story. He knew His Son would return in victory. But that does not change the loss He must have felt. God the Father sacrificed the immediate presence of Christ to send His Son to earth.

Jesus intentionally left heaven to become human. Paul gives us a glimpse of the heavy price that Jesus paid to become one of us:

> *Have this mind among yourselves, which is yours in Christ Jesus, who, though he was in the form of God, did not count equality with God a thing to be grasped, but emptied himself, by taking the form of a servant, being born in the likeness of men. Philippians 2:5-7.*

But what exactly did Christ empty Himself? What did Jesus willingly give up becoming that Child in the manger? This means Christ emptied Himself of His divine privileges of omnipotence, omniscience, and omnipresence to become a servant.

He also emptied Himself of the heavenly fellowship and glory that He shared with the Father and the Spirit. Before His arrest, Jesus prayed, "I glorified you on earth, having accomplished the work that you gave me to do. And now, Father, glorify me in your own presence with the glory that I had with you before the world existed," John 17:4–5. I think Jesus also longed for the fellowship of the Father. In my words, Christ was saying, "I want to be with You Father!"

It is hard for us to fathom the expense the Father, the Son, and the Holy Spirit paid to allow Christ to be born among us. They endured this pain to redeem us from every kindred, tongue, and tribe. But God loves us so much that He allowed this great sacrifice to bring you and me into His family. Heaven lost the glory of the Son for a season that we might receive the glory of the Son for eternity.

Heavenly Father, thank you for the price you paid for my salvation. It is hard for me to fathom how You felt when Your Son left Heaven and the pain you endured watching Your Son suffer on the cross. Forgive us Father for the pain we have caused by our sin. I now long to fellowship with You as You and Jesus and the Spirit commune together. Jesus, you lost everything for me, even Your life – I commit

DAVE HOLLAND

my life to serve You who gave so much for me.
Amen.

Day 19

The Day Earth was Filled with Music

And there were shepherds living out in the fields nearby, keeping watch over their flocks at night. An angel of the Lord appeared to them, and the glory of the Lord shone around them, and they were terrified. But the angel said to them, "Do not be afraid. I bring you good news of great joy that will be for all the people. Today in the town of David a Savior has been born to you; he is Christ the Lord. This will be a sign to you: You will find a baby wrapped in cloths and lying in a manger."

Suddenly a great company of the heavenly host appeared with the angel, praising God and saying,

"Glory to God in the highest, and on earth peace to men on whom his favor rests."
Luke 2:8-14

The shepherds were terrified when they should have been rejoicing; they were afraid when they should have had peace. Why do we react in the opposite manner we should when God does something supernatural? Are we so afraid of things originating in the spiritual realm? I remember as a young Christian when people referred to the "Holy Ghost," I always got the jitters conjuring up images of Casper or the Haunted Mansion at Disneyland. God, help me not to be afraid when You want to do something wonderful!

The shepherds are my heroes. They faithfully do their job protecting their sheep from lions and wolves. They sleep in the field because it's necessary for their flock and their families. When I grow up I want to be as faithful as them.

Can you imagine faithfully working hard at your job when a mighty host of angels start singing in your workplace? Beautiful music, heavenly worship, intoxicating melodies suddenly erupt and drown out the phones, photocopier, and elevator music. The shepherds were afraid, but I hope I would tap my foot, clap my hands and sing with them. What would you do? Too often fear robs us our joy!

This is the sign guys, *a Savior has been born to you; he is Christ the Lord, a Savior has been born to you.* The Anointed One has come to deliver us from evil and set us free. It is interesting to me that the shepherds who guarded the sheep held for sacrifice were given the announcement of the Savior who would take away the sin of the world forever. They tended sheep for sacrifice, and they proclaimed the Messiah destined for sacrifice.

Praise is the only right response. The angels got it, the shepherds received it and so should we. The Messiah has arrived to deliver us from our sins past, present, and future. This is the greatest news in history. God is for us not against us. He came because He loves us not so He could smack us down. Stand up and sing with the angels.

I began attending a place where people worshipped by raising their hands to God while they sang. When I tried this I felt so awkward, so conspicuous – as if everybody was looking at me. First

Timothy 2:8 says *I desire therefore that the men pray everywhere, lifting up holy hands, without wrath and doubting;*(NKJV). The Bible says to lift our hands toward God in prayer and worship so what was holding me back? My focus was on me – that was the problem. My mind was occupied with, *what will people think about me?* Instead of focusing on God I was afraid of what people would think. Fear was robbing me of joy just like it did the Shepherds.

What do angels look like? And what does an "angelic host" look or sound like? Awesome, I imagine. This passage has been reduced to a Hallmark Christmas Card slogan too often and that does not convey the incredible nature of the event. God went to great lengths to tell us about His Son and that His favor rests upon us.

What does His favor resting upon us mean? God's favor rests on those who believe in His Son. The Greek word for *favor* is *eudokia* meaning God's goodwill has turned toward us bringing peace, prosperity, and rest. We are blessed with God's unconditional love.

Yet our mind screams, *so why don't I feel blessed?* Yes, we struggle daily; life can be so difficult. God requires two things for us to live in the joy of His blessing. First, we must trust Him with a steadfast faith through the struggle. Second, we must be thankful for the abundance of His blessing upon our lives. Without thankfulness we will miss the miracle happening before our eyes even as the Shepherds did. A heart that is thankful sees the beauty around them., hears the angels singing, responds to God's great blessing upon us because of Jesus.

*Lord God hear my cry today – open my eyes to
Your blessings all around me, open my ears to hear
the beauty of Your song. Remove the fear that
makes me hide from you and bow to the desires of
others. Sometimes I cower before the supernatural
grace You have showered upon me like the
Shepherds who were terrified at Your demonstration
of favor. Help me to run through the storm rather
than around it. I commit to staying confident in You
because I am Yours and You are mine. Today I
receive Your Son as my Savior, Deliverer, Grace-
Giver, and my Lord, I receive all the blessings they
entail – hope, peace, prosperity, and security. Thank
YOU LORD. Amen*

Day 20

Love So Simple

When the angels had left them and gone into heaven, the
shepherds said to one another, "Let's go to Bethlehem and see this
thing that has happened, which the Lord has told us about."

So they hurried off and found Mary and Joseph, and the
baby, who was lying in the manger. When they had seen him, they
spread the word concerning what had been told them about this
child, and all who heard it were amazed at what the shepherds said
to them. But Mary treasured up all these things and pondered them
in her heart. The shepherds returned, glorifying and praising God
for all the things they had heard and seen,
which were just as they had been told.
Luke 2: 15-20

Our American notion of Christmas means little to an
eighty-year-old man living in a village in Zimbabwe. He knows
nothing of shopping malls or Christmas trees. How do you explain
Christ's birth to him?

I wonder what Christmas means to a mother who has lost
her husband, who struggles to take care of her children, stressing
every day to survive. What does Christ's birth mean to little

children with smudges on their cheeks, sparkling eyes and hunger in their bellies?

Let's look at the birth of Christ without the lens of our Western Christmas culture and see what it would say to us.

The arrival of God into our world varies in meaning for individuals, yet it is a simple message for humble people. Sometimes we are like the folks who threw a party to honor a special friend. They sent out invitations, decorated the house and prepared the food. Everyone comes at the designated time, but the guest of honor has not arrived. Finally, they realize no one invited the guest of honor. I wonder if we go through elaborate preparations yet forget whose birthday it is. Have we made Christmas all about us and not about HIM?

Luke 2:15-20 describes the birth of the Savior in all His undecorated glory. Shepherds respond to the angelic message and witness God Almighty as a baby in the cattle-yard, wrapped in rags. Shepherds were at the opposite end of the social strata from King Herod, the celebrities, and the influential people. Shepherds lived in the fields with their animals and probably smelled like them. They were disrespected and void of power or prestige. God's angel visits them announcing; *a Savior has been born to you; he is Christ the Lord.*

No matter how insignificant you may think you are, God knows you, and you are important to Him. God often reveals Himself to people the world overlooks. When God chose a mother for His Son, He skipped the fashion salons and beauty parlors. He bypassed the furs and diamond-studded-starlets. Instead, He turned to the insignificant village of Nazareth, looking for a peasant girl to mother His Child, and lowly shepherds to be His witnesses.

EVERY DAY JESUS

The trappings of Christ's birth are modest, void of an entourage of nurses and doctors. Jesus was born in a barn, wrapped in simple strips of cloth, and laid in the livestock's feeding trough. This quiet exhibition screams of God's love for the masses, for the average Joe and Mary. If God cares about shepherds and villagers, He certainly cares about you.

Most of us have known feelings of rejection, sometimes amplified by the Holiday season. God whispers to you, *No! You're wrong. I made the announcement to shepherds, and I make it to you. To YOU, a Savior is born.* Your life matters because God sees and loves you!

The second thing this passage teaches us is that life is important. Imagine those shepherds sitting around the campfire wondering if their lives have meaning, *What difference does it make if we watch the sheep or not?*

Maybe we think, *What difference does it make if I get up every morning or not? It seems as if my life is an endless cycle of work, sleep and chores. I just wonder if life is worth living at all.*

God's announcement to the shepherds says to us; *your life is worthwhile no matter who you are. It is My gift to you. Therefore, live every moment of it, because you matter to Me.* Our lives are elevated through the knowledge of Christ. Live out God's purpose for your life.

Some years ago, a newspaper cartoon pictured two farmers in Kentucky, standing in a field talking. One asked, *anything exciting happen today?*

Nah, nothing exciting, said the other farmer. *Oh, there was a baby born over at Tom Lincoln's home, but nothing exciting ever happens around here.* That baby eventually became President of the United States, changing the course of American history.

I wonder if there were people in Bethlehem on that night asking, *anything exciting happen today?*

Maybe they were told, *No, nothing much. Oh, but I heard some teenage girl gave birth to an illegitimate child in a stable, but nothing exciting ever happens around here.* It turns out that it was the most important baby in human history.

One life can make a huge difference! It's impossible to live and not influence someone. It is said that the average person influences an average of 10,000 lives during their lifetime. Dare to believe that God can use you to as His change agent. Mary believes and the incredible happened.

Shepherds lead difficult lives. When things got hard, during times of poverty, enslavement, and exile, they would dream of the Messiah. They prayed for hundreds of years, *Let the Messiah come. Let Him come today!* In times of doubt, the shepherds must have wondered, *Does God hear our prayers? Does God keep His promises? Will the Messiah ever come?* But when the angelic choir started to sing they responded in faith – they came to adore the Messiah. It is our faith and ability to respond to God that gives us special significance.

The shepherd's faith may have faltered at times, but when the announcement came to shepherds, God was saying, *Your faith matters and is not in vain. I am the God who keeps His promises. The Messiah has come.*

How about you? Sometimes you become weary. Have family burdens? Feel alone? Some Christians pray, *Come, Lord Jesus, come quickly!* Or we ask ourselves, *Why is He is waiting so long?*

One day Christ will come again. Be ready, claim your inheritance, ask God to reveal Himself to you and His purpose for your life right now. He will come for us all - shepherds and kings, wise men and peasants. He will come for His people. He'll dry our tears and take away our pain. Then we'll sing from the heart the old hymn, *It will be worth it all when we see Jesus*[3] - so clear, so divine, so simple.

Christ's birth means that the transcendent Lord of the universe becomes one of us – He is close to us. Jesus knows what it is like to wear our skin. God's love is available to all who are simple enough to receive it and worship Him every day.

Father God, I come asking You to open my ears and eyes to the Angelic message of Christ's Presence. Show me who I am in relation to Him. Renew today my hope in Christ's coming Kingdom. May I be born anew by a fresh awareness of Your Spirit moving in me. Reveal to me how You see me and how I should proclaim Your glory like the shepherds. Your will be done, Amen.

---

[3] Rusthoi, Esther Kerr. *It Will Be Worth It All.*

DAVE HOLLAND

Day 21

The Name of Jesus

On the eighth day, when it was time to circumcise him, he was named Jesus, the name the angel had given him before he had been conceived.

When the time of their purification according to the Law of Moses had been completed, Joseph and Mary took him to Jerusalem to present him to the Lord (as it is written in the Law of the Lord, "Every firstborn male is to be consecrated to the Lord"), and to offer a sacrifice in keeping with what is said in the Law of the Lord: "a pair of doves or two young pigeons."
Luke 2:21-24

John Lennon mistakenly believed the Beatles were more famous than Christ. While the dead Beatle lies in the grave, Jesus' Name is the most recognized Name in the world.

Two hundred and fifty years ago the French Enlightenment philosopher Voltaire railed against the authenticity of the Bible. He said Christianity would be extinct within a hundred years. Ironically, within a hundred years of his death, Voltaire is all but forgotten and his home now belongs to the Geneva Bible Society. That group distributes millions of Bibles from there today.

Over two billion people on this planet believe the Bible and trust the Name of Jesus for salvation, hope, and healing. His is the name that makes demons flee and believers rejoice.

Luke records the endowment of Christ's Name at the Temple in our passage today. The Name of Jesus derives from the Hebrew name Joshua meaning *The Lord is Salvation*. It is the Name world religions hate because Christians will not bow to Mohammed, Buddha, Krishna or secular humanism. The Name of Jesus represents the man above all men - God of very God, light of very light. It is the Name that sometimes divides families, communities, and nations, dividing between unbelievers and believers. It is the Name above all names, the Name to whom every knee shall bow, and every tongue confesses, *HE is LORD*.

There is power in Jesus' Name to break every chain of addiction and unclean habit. The resurrection power exerted by the Name robs the grave, strikes the Devil dumb and sends demons scurrying like lizards on hot rocks. It is the Name by which every sickness must submit, and every affliction must bow.

Jesus demolishes evil kingdoms and causes dictators to tremble. Satan shakes with terror as heaven populates with new believers. Heaven's armies engage the hordes of Hades in battle reducing that dark dominion to rubble. Lucifer's power is rendered void at the very whisper of the Name of Jesus.

It is said that Satan no longer recruits late Saturday nights at the local bars but rather he goes to church Sunday mornings and employs demons of gossip. strife and legalism to tempt the faithful. Those fellowships that lift and worship the Name of Jesus cause the devils to flee.

EVERY DAY JESUS

A multitude of biblical metaphors strive to define the Name, but it transcends reduction to letters on a page. His Name is Creator God, Mighty Deliverer, and Silent Sacrifice. He is the Captain of Angel armies, the Dayspring, Desire of the Ages, Lily of the Valley - Bright and Morning Star. He is the Suffering Messiah and the Conquering Hero. He is our Healer, our Comforter, and our Mighty Baptizer with the Holy Spirit, our Burden Bearer, and our High Priest. HE became sin for us that we might put on His Righteousness like a royal robe.

Mary and Joseph were simply giving their little boy a name. But one day, when the trumpet of God shall sound, the King with that Name will raise the dead and snatch us up to be with Him. He will parade us as trophies of His grace into the very throne room of God. Revelation 19:11-16, *NKJV,* wraps up the holy writ with these words about Him:

Behold, a white horse and He who sat on him was called Faithful and True, and in righteousness He judges and makes war. His eyes were like a flame of fire, and on His head were many crowns. He had a NAME written that no one knew except Himself. He was clothed with a robe dipped in blood, and His name is called The Word of God. And the armies in heaven, clothed in fine linen, white and clean, followed Him on white horses. Now out of His mouth goes a sharp sword, that He should strike the nations. And He Himself will rule them with a rod of iron. He Himself treads the winepress of the fierceness and wrath of Almighty God. And He has on His robe and on His thigh a name written: KING OF KINGS AND LORD OF LORDS." His name is JESUS

Do you intimately know the power of the Name of Jesus? Does your heart swell with the white-hot heat of His Presence? Is the Name of Jesus the filter through which all your life decisions are made?

Please pray with me:

My Lord, I bow to the power of Your Name. I pray that I am known by Your Name and live in the dynamic of Your Name. I ask that I could walk in Your authority this day. Empower me to live for the glory of Your Name. In Jesus Name I pray. Amen.

Day 22

A Prescription for Hope and Health

*Now there was a man in Jerusalem called Simeon, who was
righteous and devout. He was waiting for the consolation of Israel,
and the Holy Spirit was upon him. It had been revealed to him by
the Holy Spirit that he would not die before he had seen the Lord's
Christ. Moved by the Spirit, he went into the temple courts. When
the parents brought in the child Jesus to do for him what the custom
of the Law required, Simeon took him in his arms and praised
God, saying:*

*"Sovereign Lord, as you have promised,
you now dismiss your servant in peace.
For my eyes have seen your salvation,
which you have prepared in the sight of all people,
a light for revelation to the Gentiles
and for glory to your people Israel."*

*The child's father and mother marveled at what was said
about him. Then Simeon blessed them and said to Mary, his
mother: "This child is destined to cause the falling and rising of
many in Israel, and to be a sign that will be spoken against, so that
the thoughts of many hearts will be revealed. And a sword will*

DAVE HOLLAND

pierce your own soul too."
Luke 2:25-35

Most people thought the old man was crazy - certainly he was odd. Waiting in Jerusalem searching for an unknown child for years was a little creepy. Can you imagine the teenage mother and her new husband making their way to the Temple to offer the ritual sacrifice for their newborn son when suddenly the old buzzard swoops in and grabs the baby? They stand there stunned, helplessly listening to the man as he bursts into prophetic song over Baby Jesus.

The traditional church calls Simeon's song in Luke 2:29-32, *Nunc Dimittis,* which means - *Now dismiss me.* Simeon waited his entire life for the Messiah, now he was ready to die, and he wanted to go out with a song. When I grow up I want to be like Simeon.

Waiting is our least favorite pastime. Our racing minds, clanging cell phones, and nervous hands constantly seek something to fill our sense of emptiness. Here is Simeon waiting, watching, hoping. People knew him as a just man, fair, honest, and devoted to God.

Beyond that, Simeon was filled with the Holy Spirit as he waited for the Messiah. How does the Holy Spirit come *upon* someone as in verse 25? Jesus explains the coming of the Spirit *…how much more will your heavenly Father give the Holy Spirit to those who ask Him!* Luke 11:13, NKJV. Since God doesn't have a drive-through window like McDonald's, you must ask the Father for the Spirit and receive Him by faith.

Simeon believed in Christ's coming and he never gave up watching for the fulfillment of the dream God had put in his heart. Trusting, hoping, and believing in the longed-for-Messiah climaxed as Simeon held the Holy Babe in his arms. Singing for joy He exults, *My eyes have seen your salvation...a light to reveal God to the nations.* Luke2:30, 32, NLT. It was a melody for all humanity. His song reveals God in ways never seen before - gentle but piercing, vulnerable yet penetrating.

Simeon hoped, believed and saw the *Desire of all nations,* Haggai 2:7. In contrast, we have a twofold problem; we don't want to wait, and we doubt the goodness of God.

Ultimately Simeon gives the child back to his mother and prophesies, *This Child is destined for the fall and rising of many in Israel, and for a sign which will be spoken against (yes, a sword will pierce through your own soul also), that the thoughts of many hearts may be revealed.* Luke 2:34-35, NKJV. Christ divides history between BC and AD. He divides humanity into believers and unbelievers. He even divides families as some will bow to His Lordship and some won't. Christ-the-Great Divider shines His light upon our thoughts, causing many to cower in shame, or defiantly resist. Believers bow in humble repentance.

Simeon speaks to us about *how* the Lord exposes our innermost thoughts and feelings. It's not so much that God judges us, as we judge ourselves by our reaction to Jesus. The Lord will cause many to rise in faith as we share God's goodness with them. He is a life preserver cast out to all who are adrift in the vast sea of human problems. Jesus also meets great opposition as William Barclay says in his commentary on Luke, *We either surrender to Him or are at war with Him.*

What can a person do when they are old? Old-man Simeon sees, believes and receives Jesus into his arms. Similarly, you must choose to embrace Jesus, praise Him, and be filled with the Holy Spirit - this is your prescription for lifelong hope and health – even for strange old people.

Dear Lord God, give me eyes like Simeon that sees who You really are. I ask to see You today that I can praise You in Your presence. May I have the patience to wait on You even when You seem far away. I ask for the qualities of endurance and faithfulness that Simeon demonstrates. Help me to see Your subtle working in the events of my life this day and give me the vision to recognize the humble presence of Jesus wherever I go. In Jesus' Name, I pray, Amen.

Day 23

A Lovely Old Age

There was also a prophetess, Anna, the daughter of Phanuel, of the tribe of Asher. She was very old; she had lived with her husband seven years after her marriage, and then was a widow until she was eighty-four. She never left the temple but worshiped night and day, fasting and praying. Coming up to them at that very moment, she gave thanks to God and spoke about the child to all who were looking forward to the redemption of Jerusalem.

When Joseph and Mary had done everything required by the Law of the Lord, they returned to Galilee to their own town of Nazareth. And the child grew and became strong; he was filled with wisdom, and the grace of God was upon him.
Luke 2:36-40

When I was about eight years old, there was an elderly woman who lived on our street. She wore a long black dress and her hair was pulled back in a bun. She would sit on her front porch every day in a rocking chair and offer a shiny new dime to any kid who would memorize the verse of scripture she had printed on a card. It was 1962 and ten cents went a long way - it bought a double scoop ice cream cone at *Thrifty's*.

I memorized those scriptures like I was a monk. When I got that dime I felt like I hit the lottery. I may not remember all the verses today, but the picture of that kind woman is engraved on my mind. She seemed as old as God. Her silver hair and serene face gave her the lofty air of holiness. Though I admit - her dimes influenced my newfound devotion to scripture memorization.

Luke 2:36-38 recounts another elderly woman by the name of *Anna the Prophetess.* She was somewhere between eighty-four and a hundred and four years old. She had known both happiness and sorrow - the husband of her youth died after only seven years of marriage. Anna responded to her grief by giving her life to God for decades of fasting and prayer. Waiting on God for the promised Messiah was the essence of her life.

I'm sure she had seen hundreds of thousands of people enter the Temple area. Conquering heroes, prophets, and kings had all paraded through during those years. Anna longed for the Messiah who would be the consolation of her people.

No one expected Anna to really find the Savior, but as the old, wrinkled woman trolled the vast courtyard, she found Mary and Jesus and erupted with praise. She discovered Him from among the multitudes because she had the quality of faith that discerned HIS presence.

What is the meaning that we can derive from Anna's life? What does she show our youth-obsessed culture? Eighty-four years young she lived for God without a facelift, collagen injection, or magical youth producing makeup. She had the inward, pristine beauty that comes from knowing the living God.

Once a person learns to dwell in the presence of God, there is a subtle transfer of His glory, a beauty that supersedes all others. Old age is not a curse - it is a refiner - something to behold and admire. Maturity and experience are the price of wisdom, but they are also an invitation to develop godliness without carrying around all the anchors of youth - ambition, lust, and the endless search for attractiveness.

Anna pulled back the blanket from Christ's face and gasped as she gazed into the face of joy personified. She found happiness when she looked into His eyes. Finally, she comprehended her history and unveiled her destiny. Dare to imagine such a moment for you!

The prophetess knew both loneliness and sorrow, yet Anna was not bitter. Sorrow can send you in one of two directions; it can make you bitter, resentful and rebellious against God, or it can make you kinder, nobler, and sympathetic to others. If you think of God as unfair, you will grow offended, but if you think of God as loving, you will trust and rest in His care. The choice is yours.

Anna's age did not hinder her expression of life because she never ceased hoping. This lady shows us God is not distant and is never late. She understands God is intimately connected to who we are, and we can confidently expect fulfillment. Anna never ceased to worship. She spent her life in God's house with God's people in authentic prayer. Old age can be for us as it was for Anna - the most glorious time of life.

My God, I pray for persistence in prayer today, the same quality of resolve that Anna displayed. I need discernment to comprehend Your Presence near me. May I also 'tell everyone around' who Jesus is! May

DAVE HOLLAND

my age develop wisdom, in the Name of the Father,
Amen.

Day 24

Human

Every year his parents went to Jerusalem for the Feast of the Passover. When he was twelve years old, they went up to the Feast, according to the custom. After the Feast was over, while his parents were returning home, the boy Jesus stayed behind in Jerusalem, but they were unaware of it. Thinking he was in their company, they traveled on for a day. Then they began looking for him among their relatives and friends. When they did not find him, they went back to Jerusalem to look for him. After three days they found him in the temple courts, sitting among the teachers, listening to them and asking them questions. Everyone who heard him was amazed at his understanding and his answers. When his parents saw him, they were astonished. His mother said to him, "Son, why have you treated us like this? Your father and I have been anxiously searching for you."

"Why were you searching for me?" he asked. "Didn't you know I had to be in my Father's house?" But they did not understand what he was saying to them.

Then he went down to Nazareth with them and was obedient to them. But his mother treasured all these things in her heart. And Jesus grew in wisdom and stature, and in favor with God and men.

Luke 2:39-52

Have you ever met anyone more precocious than an adolescent boy? We find in Luke 2:39-52 the boy Jesus, who is intelligent and articulate. He was fully human – just like us yet so much more. Christ was also God in every way. Nevertheless, He laid aside His divine privileges becoming one of us completely. He bled; He cried, He grew from childhood to manhood with our aches and pains.

The Greeks and Romans idealized the human mind and body to the point of self-worship. We do much the same things in our workout spas with endless mirrors, our worship of the celebrity cult, and our body enhancement industry. The problem is we never seem to achieve perfection.

Christ epitomized the essence of the ideal human and demonstrated God's original design for us. He touched us, heard us, felt our emotions, and saw our flaws. He was born a squalling infant and passed flawlessly through adolescence to adulthood, yet with one huge difference from us – He did not have the inclination to sin.

Can you imagine what it would be like growing up unpolluted with temptation? No nagging lust to hound your thoughts, no pride undermining your motivation, and no covetousness driving you with the endless desire for more. Christ was certainly tempted as we are according to Hebrews 4:15 yet He would not allow them to take up residence in His mind.

Jesus was free of these terrible burdens and showed us what God the Father intended for humanity. Luke 2:39-52 pulls back the curtain giving us a glimpse of Christ's early years, and in the process shows us the great potential we possess.

A Jewish boy was considered a man when he turned twelve years of age. He became a *son of the Law* with the opportunity and obligation to learn the scriptures. In Christ's first visit to the Temple as a young man of twelve years, we find Him *listening and asking questions*. Jesus engaged His mind and heart, learning and becoming everything God desired Him to be.

Christ grappled with the scriptures and probed the best teachers in the land. He astonished the scholars because His mind was clear, bright and focused. Could it be that this was when He discovered He was the Son of God? Revelation comes to those whose heart seeks knowledge. I believe that in the process of engaging the scriptures, we discover who we are.

We can learn who God created us to be by engaging the scriptures as Christ did. If we will lay aside the things that encumber us it is amazing how much knowledge we can absorb. More than that, we will be astonished at who we become.

Sandwiched between the two commendations of Christ as *growing in favor with God and man* is the story of Jesus' wayward delay at the Temple. Mary seemed to scream, *How could you do that to us, Jesus?* Most parents would feel the same way if their child left the family without notice to stay in the church for two days. But such was the hunger that Jesus had for the scriptures.

This passage concludes with Jesus obeying His earthly parents. His compliance embraces wisdom, and His obedience warms the heart of any parent. When Luke writes of Jesus' relationship to Joseph and Mary in Luke 2:51, he uses the Greek word *hupotasso* to describe the parent-child relationship. This word implies power brought under control. Christ was the Son of God and Creator of all things but while He was in the flesh this young man respectfully submitted to His parent's authority. Jesus went to Jerusalem as a child but went home as a man, yet, He still submitted to His parents.

All living things grow. Human learning potential is immense. Our humanity and spirituality are directly tied to our ability to grasp knowledge and mature. Will we grow up spiritually to become fully human and everything God created us to be?

Dear Jesus, grant me the holy hunger You had to grow and learn. Help me recover my God-design. I ask You to give me mentors and teachers who help me discover all that You are so I can become all that You created me to be. Please reveal Yourself to me and grant me the desire to want more of You. I pray this in Your Name, Amen.

Day 25

Help Me, God!

In the fifteenth year of the reign of Tiberius Caesar - when Pontius Pilate was governor of Judea, Herod tetrarch of Galilee, his brother Philip tetrarch of Iturea and Traconitis, and Lysanias tetrarch of Abilene - during the high priesthood of Annas and Caiaphas, the word of God came to John son of Zechariah in the desert. He went into all the country around the Jordan, preaching a baptism of repentance for the forgiveness of sins. As is written in the book of the words of Isaiah the prophet:

"A voice of one calling in the desert, 'Prepare the way for the Lord, make straight paths for him.

Every valley shall be filled in,
every mountain and hill made low.

The crooked roads shall become straight,
the rough ways smooth.

And all mankind will see God's salvation.'"
Luke 3:1-6

Here comes John the Baptist interrupting our happy thoughts again. He appears in the Gospels with eyes blazing, pointing his gnarly finger and shouting damnation. Why does the

103

good news of the gospel start with a weirdo wearing camel hair and shouting *Repent?*

John the Baptist is an uncomfortable figure, so disturbing that we cannot ignore him. Just as we begin to celebrate Christmas with thoughts of *Joy to the world* and *Peace on earth,* this fire-breathing oddball brands us as a *brood of vipers.*

Have you ever seen John the Baptist in a Nativity scene or a Christmas pageant? Nope, yet even as we are setting up manger scenes in the church, John sneaks up in our gospel readings casting gloom and guilt. John's message glares at us through the lights and trappings of our churches. God uses this man to reveal a most remarkable message - he guides us back to God.

Preacher David C. Fisher says, *We want to feel good about ourselves and we expect our religion to serve our every need. Guilt and personal responsibility are out of fashion and sin is a bad word, the bad news of bad religion. We want good news only. We want to sing 'Away in the Manger,' and instead, the Church sends us a wild-eyed, locust-eating prophet.* [4]

John won't go away. He opens each of the four Gospels with a significant key - before God initiates something new, He first calls us to repentance. Notice the first word out of John's mouth in Matthew 3:2, *Repent.*

Look at the first declaration from Jesus in Matthew 4:17, *Repent.*

On the day of Pentecost, Peter stands up and declares, *Repent.* Repentance is a primary theme in the Bible and the first word of the Christian life.

---

[4] Fisher, David C.; *The Library of Distinctive Sermons, Volume 2* page 169

EVERY DAY JESUS

J. I. Packer notes, *Christians are called to a life of repentance, as a discipline integral to healthy holy living. The first of Luther's ninety-five theses, nailed to the Wittenberg church door in 1517 declared, 'When our Lord and Master Jesus Christ said, 'Repent,' He willed that the whole life of believers should be one of repentance.'*[5]

Why is repentance so important? The Hebrew word for repentance presents a picture that gives us a visual clue - it means to reverse your direction in life. Repentance directs us to turn away from a self-centered life and open our hearts toward God saying, *Help me, God.* Make no mistake - repentance is not a simple apology or even a formal confession – it is a change of life.

Sin isn't just deeds you do, words you say, or thoughts you think. Evil comes from deep within us pushing us away from God's best. The root of our lostness is the issue we must confront. I'm sure you know what I mean — that reservoir of bitterness deep in our soul, that well of anger stored in the center of our life. There is a place in your heart where doubt lives - resentment smolders, and all manner of evil brews. We must turn from those dark alleys to follow Jesus on the road to eternal life.

Jesus calls us all to radical change, and repentance is the starting point. Salvation is free, but change is never easy.

Jesus didn't come primarily to make us feel good about ourselves. He came to save us *from ourselves.* He wants to change us at precisely the place we resist conversion, and the Lord wants to birth something new in us at that place. The birth process screams with the labor pains of a heartfelt moral inventory leading to

---

[5] Packer, J.I.; *Classic Collection, Daily Readings for Your Spiritual Journey.* Page 78. NavPress, Colorado Springs, Colorado.

repentance - just ask John the Baptist. He reminds us to fall on our knees and cry out, *Help me, God.*

Father, I come to You as a sinner saved by Your grace. May I have the courage to repent of the sin that lurks within me. Flush my soul of the toxins that clog my spirit. I give my faults to You and ask that You help me to live a life that is victorious and glorifying to You. Straighten my paths that I can live with integrity and honor. I pray desperately that I will have good fruit to lay at Your feet when I meet You face to face. In Christ's Name, I pray, Amen.

Day 26

The Test of True Faith

John said to the crowds coming out to be baptized by him, "You brood of vipers! Who warned you to flee from the coming wrath? Produce fruit in keeping with repentance. And do not begin to say to yourselves, 'We have Abraham as our father.' For I tell you that out of these stones God can raise up children for Abraham. The ax is already at the root of the trees, and every tree that does not produce good fruit will be cut down and thrown into the fire."

"What should we do then?" the crowd asked.

John answered, "The man with two tunics should share with him who has none, and the one who has food should do the same."

Tax collectors also came to be baptized. "Teacher," they asked, "what should we do?"

"Don't collect any more than you are required to," he told them.

Then some soldiers asked him, "And what should we do?"

He replied, "Don't extort money and don't accuse people falsely - be content with your pay."

The people were waiting expectantly and were all wondering in their hearts if John might possibly be the Christ. John answered them all, "I baptize you with water. But one more powerful than I will come, the thongs of whose sandals I am not worthy to untie. He will baptize you with the Holy Spirit and with fire. His winnowing fork is in his hand to clear his threshing floor and to gather the wheat into his barn, but he will burn up the chaff with unquenchable fire." And with many other words John exhorted the people and preached the good news to them.

But when John rebuked Herod the tetrarch because of Herodias, his brother's wife, and all the other evil things he had done, Herod added this to them all: He locked John up in prison.
Luke 3:7-20

John the Baptist brings us a special message via Luke 3. This Word is especially relevant for those who are not Jews. John speaks directly to Gentiles about how to open their hearts and turn back to God.

Relating to John as *a voice of one crying in the wilderness: prepare the way of the Lord,* Luke strikes up the tune of Greco/Roman pageantry. The arrival of a conqueror or king required a certain protocol that Luke describes carefully.

Imagine that you are a Greek or Roman citizen in the first century with only a vague recollection of an obscure group of Jews living in the far reaches of the empire. A letter comes to you from a respected physician and historian named Luke describing a new religion. He paints the picture of a God-King coming to with the royal pageantry you would expect.

Luke depicts John the Baptist far differently than Matthew, who recounts a wild-eyed prophet preaching to the Jews in the manner of an Old Testament *prophet*. Nor does Luke take the approach of the evangelist John, who described the Baptist as a *witness* of Christ. No, Luke gives six historic secular reference points of John's ministry placing him hot on the Greco/Roman news wire as a true King. He was saying, *this man's words are vital to you now whoever you are!* The emergence of John the Baptist is the hinge on which history turns.

In ancient times when a king proposed to tour a region of his domain, he sent a messenger to tell the people to level the roads and fill the potholes to make a nice, smooth road - *make way for the King*. Luke thereby introduces John the Baptist as the courier of the King, and in doing so, Luke connects with everyone in the empire. He is explaining how to make way for the coming spiritual King Jesus. They had seen Caesars parade through the realm with great pomp for centuries. But the preparation of which John insisted was a cultivation of the heart. He was saying, *The King is coming, mend your hearts and fill the potholes in your lives.*

John's message goes still deeper. He was also speaking to Jews who thought they had special privileges with God. Misguided by their national pride, they thought Gentiles would be judged by another, harsher standard. Up to that point, water baptism was only for new converts to Judaism. Imagine their shock when they heard John call the Jews to repentance and baptism. John virtually shouted to his Jewish listeners to be baptized for the forgiveness of sins while they mistakenly assumed they were already forgiven.

One can almost hear the Greek readers saying, *Amen Luke, those self-righteous Jews need a little humbling.* The message was also clear to the Gentiles to whom Luke was writing that the door was now open to God through sincere repentance and baptism.

The readers were surely stunned by John's forthrightness. Luke's account draws the readers into the meat of the message. True repentance requires an authenticity that produces positive change. For instance, let him who has more than he needs share with those who don't. Tax Collectors should be honest and not steal from the people, but rather they should be content with their pay. True Christianity changes our behavior. It makes quality husbands who honor their wives and wives who respect their husbands. It makes us better parents and dependable employees. Real Christianity makes us compassionate toward others serving their needs above our own.

This teaching was Synagogue 101 for the Christian Jews and a news flash for Gentiles. The Baptist commands them to DO what the Word of God decreed. The Gentile readers must have exclaimed, *Wow, a religion that expects people to live out what they believe.* In the end, true faith produces fruit for God and is measured by what you live out in the day-to-day struggles of life. Do you have fruit to lay at the Master's feet?

Dear Lord, I ask You to bend my heart to Your kingdom's demands. I want to live in a manner that is honest and glorifying to You. I confess my need for Your help. Thank You for Your direction and clarity concerning where I need to make changes. I long to hear Your words, "well done good and faithful servant. In Jesus' Name, I pray, Amen.

Day 27

The Poor Man's Sacrifice

When all the people were being baptized, Jesus was baptized
too. And as he was praying, heaven was opened and the Holy
Spirit descended on him in bodily form like a dove. And a voice
came from heaven: "You are my Son, whom I love;
with you I am well pleased."
Luke 3:21-22

We think doves are symbols of peace on earth. We often use them as emblems of genteel love shared between couples on their wedding day. In reality, doves are simply white pigeons, dirty birds that crap all over everything.

The ancients did not share our romanticized notions about pigeons. Rather, the Bible prescribed these common birds as the poor man's sacrifice, an acceptable, inexpensive substitute for a lamb or a bull to kill in religious rituals. Bam! Here comes the Holy Spirit at this critical moment in Jesus' life, floating down out of the sky *like a dove.*

It strikes me as important that as Jesus was baptized He prayed, and heaven opened. Heaven didn't open to let the little birdie out - the heavenly realm broke open. Something mighty happened in response to Christ's obedience in baptism, access to God was opened.

Jesus PRAYED and the Holy Spirit descended, anointing Him with power and grace. He was as reliant on God's Spirit as we are. As He was praying - heaven shook - and the Spirit began to move.

Make no mistake about it – to the people who witnessed this event, the bird spoke of the poor man's sacrifice as common as pennies in your pocket. This spiritual anointing is for every believer – rich or poor, bond or free, male or female.

When the Holy Spirit arrived, God spoke with words that Jesus already knew. Every person must hear this word in their heart of hearts, *You are My beloved Son; in You, I am well pleased.* It is that *Voice* that gives each of us our eternal identity and significance. Most people crave hearing such defining and encouraging words. I believe God's people are here to be the Voice of God speaking acceptance to the world and one to another.

Speak God-words of loving affirmation to the people you meet!

I challenge you to an experiment. The next time you go to a restaurant and the waiter delivers your order, they will typically ask, *Is there anything else?*

Try answering with these words, *You are God's child.* Then, watch what happens as the Holy Spirit arrives confirming God's love. You will see a person soften and melt (occasionally resist) before your eyes. Ask them if you can pray for them. Most often people answer with a resounding *Yes!* God spoke uniquely to His own Son, but the model is true for us as well.

EVERY DAY JESUS

Many years ago, I traveled to Toronto, Canada with a group of men. There was a tremendous revival occurring there, and we wanted to witness it. Exceptional signs of God's presence along with unique healings were occurring.

Following the message, we worshiped for hours as hundreds of people waited in lines for prayer. God touched many people that night and our men had many testimonies of God's goodness. I waited in line for prayer feeling a little dejected, wondering why God hadn't done anything miraculous to me.

Finally, the ministry leaders came down my line and prayed for me, I felt nothing, nada, zippo, zilch. But after the prayer team passed on, without warning, I heard a very soft voice deep in my heart - actually, it was three voices blended - God the Father's, my father's, and my voice saying, *I love you, my son.* At that moment, a lifetime of hurt was healed.

My prayer for you today is that you will hear the still, small voice of the Father speaking His love and acceptance to you. Jesus *IS* the poor man's sacrifice. He opened the heavens for us that the Holy Spirit might work in our lives baptizing us in the Father's love and affirming us as his children.

Jesus said in John 10 that His sheep know His voice. Most people don't hear God's voice because they are afraid of what He will say, or they are too busy to listen. Fear not my friend, God wants to speak – He wants to lite upon you as a gentle dove and say that you are His beloved child, the apple of His eye.

Father, I come to You in obedience today believing that You want to baptize me with your Spirit of love and power. Enable me to hear Your loving Voice and to speak Your gracious words like Jesus Your Son. Heal the deep hurts in my heart, satisfy the longing in my soul, and help me to slow down enough to hear Your voice. Praying for the Dove to come upon me, Amen.

Day 28

The Zig-Zag Path of Life

Now Jesus himself was about thirty years old when he began his ministry. He was the son, so it was thought, of Joseph, the son of Heli, the son of Matthat, the son of Levi, the son of Melki, the son of Jannai, the son of Joseph, the son of Mattathias, the son of Amos, the son of Nahum, the son of Esli, the son of Naggai, the son of Maath, the son of Mattathias, the son of Semein, the son of Josech, the son of Joda, the son of Joanan, the son of Rhesa, the son of Zerubbabel, the son of Shealtiel, the son of Neri, the son of Melki, the son of Addi, the son of Cosam, the son of Elmadam, the son of Er, the son of Joshua, the son of Eliezer, the son of Jorim, the son of Matthat, the son of Levi, the son of Simeon, the son of Judah, the son of Joseph, the son of Jonam, the son of Eliakim, the son of Melea, the son of Menna, the son of Mattatha, the son of Nathan, the son of David, the son of Jesse, the son of Obed, the son of Boaz, the son of Salmon, the son of Nahshon, the son of Amminadab, the son of Ram, the son of Hezron, the son of Perez, the son of Judah, the son of Jacob, the son of Isaac, the son of Abraham, the son of Terah, the son of Nahor, the son of Serug, the son of Reu, the son of Peleg, the son of Eber, the son of Shelah, the son of Cainan, the son of Arphaxad, the son of Shem, the son of Noah, the son of Lamech, the son of Methuselah, the son of Enoch,

the son of Jared, the son of Mahalalel, the son of Kenan, the son of Enosh, the son of Seth, the son of Adam, the son of God.
Luke 3:23-38

So and so begat so and so who begat so and so, blah, blah, blah! Genealogies seem as boring as nuts and bolts in a hardware store. Everybody has a genealogy but who really cares?

You should care. There are two days that are of supreme importance in each person's life – the day you were born and the day you discover *why* you were born.

Your ancestors matter, they passed to you the essential DNA that makes you who you are. Jesus' genealogy gave Him His physical characteristics through His mother's line, His legal qualifications through HIs father's line, and His Spiritual essence through the Seed of the Holy Spirit. He was fully human and fully divine.

Matthew recounts Christ's lineage starting with Abraham, father of the Hebrew people, and descends to Jesus' birth through the line of Mary, thus showing His purity of Jewish lineage. His genealogy includes some notable women and is indicative of the Jewish cultural belief that a person's religion is usually passed on through the woman.

Luke's genealogy starts with the birth of Christ and works backward through Joseph's line all the way to Adam, the father of the human race. Why the difference between the two gospels? Luke was writing to show Christ's affinity for all peoples and emphasizes His humanness. True to his Gentile origin, Luke sees Jesus as the Man among all men, Savior of all peoples.

Woven into the fabric of Christ's heritage lays a beautiful yet sordid tale. Jesus' heritage is not as pristine as one might imagine. It includes no less than two prostitutes (Tamar and Rahab), at least two adulterers (Judah and David), a floozy exhibitionist (Bathsheba), a murderer (David), a drunkard (Noah), and Solomon, whose sins are too varied to categorize.

Christ's heritage confirms the adage that says everyone has a past - legacies marred with regret. It also speaks to the misgivings many of us carry about our responses to the events of our lives. The fact that God managed to enter the bloodline of sinful people and seed it with His own sinless Son gives us hope that God can infuse our negative history with new life.

Truly - prophets, priests, and kings also populate Christ's ancestral line giving him a heritage unlike any other. Saturated with divinity and motivated by grace, Jesus comes to us through a foreordained footprint. His song is syncopated with love and moved by the melody of the Spirit - a song that demons loathe and angels long to hear. His is a song written for you.

For there is born to you this day in the city of David a Savior, who is Christ the Lord. And this will be the sign to you: You will find a Babe wrapped in swaddling cloths, lying in a manger. And suddenly there was with the angel a multitude of the heavenly host praising God and saying: "Glory to God in the highest, and on earth peace, goodwill toward men!" Luke 2:11-14, NKJV.

Christ's lineage miraculously synthesizes God and man. It includes us when we are born-again. Max Lucado says in his masterful book, *Grace - This is the gift that God gives, A grace that grants us first the power to receive love and then the power to give it. A grace that changes us, shapes us and leads us to a life that is eternally altered.* [6]

When you put your faith in Jesus you are entering that legacy of grace. You are woven into the family of God and become part of the genealogy of God. He claims you as His child and He becomes your Father of Fathers.

Will you pass on this legacy freely given by God? Will you receive the goodwill and grace poured out to you through the Holy Spirit? The birth of Jesus was the ultimate sign of God's kindness toward us, inviting us into His eternal family. Christ is God's gift to you, a package wrapped in humble humanity, ribboned by His blood and topped with the bow of goodwill toward you.

Father, I come to You as Your child. I choose this day to worship You alone. Shape my life today even as you formed Jesus' human lineage. I receive Your embrace as a full-fledged family member. Thank You for including me in Your loving fellowship. In Christ's Name, I pray, Amen.

[6] Lucado, Max; *Grace: More Than We Deserved, Greater Than We imagined.* Published by Thomas Nelson, 2012, Nashville, Tennessee.

Day 29

The Lure of Temptation

Jesus, full of the Holy Spirit, returned from the Jordan and was led by the Spirit in the desert, where for forty days he was tempted by the devil. He ate nothing during those days, and at the end of them he was hungry.

The devil said to him, "If you are the Son of God, tell this stone to become bread."

Jesus answered, "It is written: 'Man does not live on bread alone."

The devil led him up to a high place and showed him in an instant all the kingdoms of the world. And he said to him, "I will give you all their authority and splendor, for it has been given to me, and I can give it to anyone I want to. So if you worship me, it will all be yours."

Jesus answered, "It is written: 'Worship the Lord your God and serve him only."

The devil led him to Jerusalem and had him stand on the highest point of the temple. "If you are the Son of God," he said, "throw yourself down from here. For it is written:

'He will command his angels concerning you to guard you carefully; they will lift you up in their hands, so that you will not strike your foot against a stone."

*Jesus answered, "It says:
'Do not put the Lord your God to the test.'"*

When the devil had finished all this tempting, he left him until an opportune time.
Luke 4:1-13

Forty days Jesus ate nothing while alone in a wilderness so desolate it was named *Jeshimun,* meaning *devastation.* Afterward, he was hungry. It is in our weakest moments that the devil comes to tempt us, and it is those moments that reveal who we are.

Christ was tempted in every way yet was without sin according to Hebrews 4:15. Aside from His sinlessness, He was not merely simulating humanity - Jesus was human in every way. The tests He suffered, the hunger He felt, and the pain He endured were tangible. He became one of us, so He could feel what we feel and show us the way to victory over our trials. Jesus was tested by the devil, the world, and the flesh just as we are. He demonstrates God's plan for ultimate victory.

I am comforted by the revelation that Christ was tempted for it reminds me that I am not alone in the fight. I have a sympathetic companion named *Jesus* with me everywhere I go – no matter how deep, dark, or ugly the circumstances – I'm never alone and neither are you.

Knowing there is a devil named *Satan* is one of the more difficult aspects of the Christian faith, yet the evidence around us is abundantly clear. From Hitler to atom bombs to Osama Bin Laden, the indications from history suggest that an evil pervades the world that is so depraved it cannot have a human origin.

Luke 4 shows both the methods and mechanisms of the devil. Satan wants to control us using illicit offers of comfort, power, and glory. The devil gives counterfeit promises of money, sex and fame to many. Jesus shows us how to resist Him and his temptations.

Christ defeats the power of darkness by first obeying the leading of the Holy Spirit. Then, He wields the power of the Word of God to crush Satan's lies. Demonic lures are no match for the Lord.

The devil must have thought he was tempting Christ in His weakest possible moment. While Jesus was weak in His body – thirsty, hungry, tired, and dirty – yet, He was strong in the Spirit. It's a contradiction that every Christian must master. Choosing to deprive our body of food fortifies our faith toward God, and it gives us a stronger resistance against the evil one. In those times that seem most difficult, God is at work in our lives strengthening us for victory.

It occurs to me that the devil never denies himself of anything. I think that he laughs at those of us who do. We must learn to fast from food and other comforts during special times in our lives to fortify us against temptation. Fasting can be fraught with pitfalls if we are not aware of the wily darts of the devil. I submit to you - this period can also be our greatest period of growth.

During Christ's temptation, He fully knew that He was God's Son yet He withstood the onslaughts of Satan as a mere man. Led by the Holy Spirit and full of the Word of God He showed us how to win. Significantly, the author of Hebrews concludes, *Because he himself suffered when he was tempted, he is able to help those who are being tempted,* Heb. 2:18.

Your character is composed of your choices. If you resist the devil, he will flee from you - if you call upon Christ, He will come to your aid – that simple. The pathway to victory over temptation always travels through Jesus, the Word, the Spirit, and your choice to cooperate with the Lord.

In my teenage years, I was invited to attend a Christian youth camp. While there I met a beautiful young lady named Leanne, who responded to my attempts to get her attention. My ego swelled, and I swaggered about the camp all day with her until it was time to go to the required evening revival meeting.

As we approached the chapel some of Leanne's friends whispered into her ear that they wanted to ditch the service and go out into the woods. She relayed the invitation to me, and I was sorely tempted to go with them. But the Holy Spirit tugged at my heart through my conscience, and I said we should go into the service.

Leanne rejected my lead, and they walked away without me, giggling as they went. My ears burned with embarrassment as I realized they were laughing at me. I look back now, and I realize that it was a small test – who was I going to serve - God or my ego?

The tests we experience are the material that forms the substance of our spiritual beings. Each choice we make adds a building block to our lives or erodes the foundation we are trying to build. Will we construct our lives with concrete blocks provided by the Word of God and the Holy Spirit or will we watch our lives shift like a sandy seashore? Jesus made His intentions clear to the devil and us – we must worship God and Him alone.

Lord Jesus, I wait on You today and ask You build something strong in me. I want more of You! I believe that You are leading me to victory over all temptations, tests, and trials. Please bring Your Word to my mind in the moments when I don't know what to do. Give me the wisdom to respond to the enticements of the enemy with scripture as You did. I thank You for being with me when the evil one attacks and through all the events of my life.
In the Name of the Father, I pray, Amen.

DAVE HOLLAND

Day 30

The Parable of the Good Life

When the devil had finished all this tempting, he left him until an opportune time.

Jesus returned to Galilee in the power of the Spirit, and news about him spread through the whole countryside. He taught in their synagogues, and everyone praised him.
Luke 4:13-15

The man's life was pleasant. So too was his worship. But, God was not pleased, so he allowed the man's life to become difficult. The man responded, *"How could this happen to me?"*

Beneath the shock, the man was smug and proud. He comforted himself by saying, "I've got this, it *will soon pass, God knows I'm trying,"* and his worship remained shallow. God soon allowed more disagreeable things to happen.

The man tried to handle his frustrations well, *"I will be patient,"* he resolved. Thinking that a good life was owed to him, he reasoned, *"God will make things pleasant again, that's His job."* His worship became a way to convince God to provide a satisfying life.

God pulled back the hedge of protection around the man a little farther. The man's life became miserable, and he got angry. God seemed to him indifferent and uncaring. Heaven's doors felt like they were slammed shut. The man could think only of better times, the good old days. His highest dreams were a return to those days, to the pleasant life he once knew.

God was not pleased. So, he allowed the man's trials to continue and his pain to remain unabated. God kept his distance from the man. He provided no comfort, no tangible reason to hope. It was difficult for God not to make everything better in the man's life, but God had a greater dream for the man than simply a return to a comfortable life. He wanted the man to find true joy, to restore his focus on what mattered most.

The deluge of doubt filling the man's soul was suffocating. All that remained was fear, anxiety, frustration, and mystery. Where was the Lord? He seemed to be gone, and life made no sense. Was God there or not? Did He even care?

The man's saving grace was that he would not give up on God. Out of the residue of his memory rose the story of Jacob wrestling with God all night in Genesis 32:23-26. Faith rose in the man's heart. He chose to fight through his doubt and despair to wrestle for God's blessing. But he fought in the dark, a darkness so deep that he gave up his dream of the easy life. For the first time in a long time, he heard his heart crying, *"Bless me, Lord, not because I am good, but because You are good. Not because I deserve Your blessing, but because it is Your nature to bless, I appeal only to Your goodness."* And why did God wrestle with the man? God longed to touch him and to reveal the only true goodness - Himself.

The man still had pain, but now he saw God. His cry for blessing was no longer a demand for a pleasant life but rather a cry for God's presence. The man felt something different - the fruit of humility was growing in him. Finally, he forgot himself and discovered his heart's hunger for God.

Then, he felt it, something like fresh water bubbling up from a spring deep in the desert of his soul. This gave rise to a new dream of knowing God intimately. His spirit was rejuvenated, he felt at home in his soul. His sufferings had created an undeniable, irresistible knocking at God's door. The man finally worshiped God for who He is, he found God to be greater than all his troubles, problems and pain. And God was pleased.

"I know you inside and out, and find little to my liking. You're not cold, you're not hot...You're stale...Here's what I want you to do: buy your gold from me, gold that's been through the refiner's fire. Then you'll be rich."
Rev. 3:15-17 (the Message)

My Lord, forgive me for the years I have lingered in the valley of the lukewarm - waiting for You to bless my efforts, as if You exist to serve my desires. I repent today and give my life to You in order to become a faithful servant of Yours. I turn to You now hungry for the zeal and power to serve You mightily, to serve you as Jesus did in the power of the Holy Spirit. "Years I spent in vanity and pride," the old song goes — it may have well been written about me. But I resist that temptation in Jesus' Name, and I open myself to the overflowing presence of the Holy Spirit. May I walk today as Jesus walked, in the power of Your Spirit, attending to your purposes. Amen.

Day 31

The Undercurrent of the Spirit

Jesus returned to Galilee in the power of the Spirit, and news about him spread through the whole countryside. He taught in their synagogues, and everyone praised him.

He went to Nazareth, where he had been brought up, and on the Sabbath day he went into the synagogue, as was his custom. And he stood up to read. The scroll of the prophet Isaiah was handed to him. Unrolling it, he found the place where it is written: "The Spirit of the Lord is on me...
Luke 4: 14-18a

My wife, Jonie, surprised me with the most wonderful gift for my sixtieth birthday. She reserved a vacation home for us, our children, and grandchildren by Lake Winnipesaukee in New Hampshire. Little did I realize the harrowing experience that would transpire.

We rented a pontoon boat for the day and ventured out on the calm, massive lake with six of our granddaughters on board. Eventually, the girls wanted to get out and swim. We anchored the boat, and I went into the water before the kids to be sure the children would be safe. That's when I made my first mistake.

I trusted my history as a strong swimmer in my youth and dove into the seemingly calm water without a life jacket. The strong undercurrent swiftly swept me away from the boat. When I made my second mistake – trying to swim against the current back to the boat - I wore myself out within minutes.

My heart pounded, and my lungs screamed for more air as the boat faded from view. While the granddaughters screamed, *Papa Dave!*, I could faintly see Jonie calmly pulling up the anchor in the boat.

I hollered with my last breath, *Forget the anchor! Just come and get me!!*

Fortunately for me, Jonie knew boats far better than me. As soon as she hauled in the anchor the boat rapidly drifted toward me - within moments, it was within reach. Jonie could save me because she knew the power of the undercurrent.

Jesus lives in the current of the Spirit, and this passage reveals how the Holy Spirit swept Jesus into His synagogue in Nazareth. Everything was the same in His childhood hometown, but Christ was different – the anointing of the Holy Spirit propelled Jesus forward toward His destiny. What did Jesus do in the synagogue? Pick up the Word of God.

Christ lived in tumultuous times with unrestrained enemies, yet He could stay in the flow of the Holy Spirit because of three personal disciplines. We live in hazardous times as well, and we can learn from Jesus' example.

Luke shows us that after Jesus had fasted and prayed, He was tested by the Devil. Then He returned *home* to His *synagogue*. As early as 300 BC the synagogue evolved as a local center of religious life for Jews. God's people assembled there for worship, prayer and the reading of the scriptures. The synagogue is where we find Jesus on the Lord's Day – worship was His priority.

The synagogue is comparable to the Christian Church for New Testament believers - it is the place of assembly to worship God.

We must accept the fact that all His life Jesus attended synagogue worship *as was His custom* (4:16). Synagogue worshippers in Jesus' day weren't any better than church-goers in ours. They, too, were proud, petty, vain, hypocritical, and sometimes rejected the people who needed God the most. But Jesus didn't distance Himself from the fellowship – He embraced it. The Son of God Himself attended synagogue faithfully and identified Himself with the People of God on earth.

Hebrews 10:25 exhorts us, *Let us not give up meeting together* (Greek - *episynagogē*), *as some are in the habit of doing, but let us encourage one another – and all the more as you see the Day approaching.* Attending worship with people was an anchor for Jesus' soul, and it must be for us as well.

Luke shows us another huge foundation stone of Christ's life – the Word of God.

Christ fought the devil off with scripture phrases from deep in His soul and close to His lips. He uttered over and over, *It is written…* In His synagogue, Jesus stands up, out of respect for the scriptures, and receives the huge scrolls of the Prophet Isaiah. He finds *the place where it is written: The Spirit of the Lord is on me…*

Jesus was the living embodiment of God's Word, and yet He still finds God's Word to Him and for Him. We need to develop that same skill - that same familiarity with the scriptures -

so that we can turn to a passage, point to it and say, *this scripture speaks to and about me.*

Hebrews 1:3 says that Christ *upholds all things by the word of His power.* God's Word holds the Christian life together. Our lives are purified, solidified and clarified by regular reading of the Bible. The Word was an anchor for Christ's soul, and it should be for ours too.

The Word and Worship drive Christ's mission like a raging river rushing down a mountain. Tomorrow's devotional details the third discipline that drove Christ's life to extraordinary places.

Holy Spirit, I worship You, Jesus and the Father today because You are so worthy. I ask You to speak to me through Your Word, sometimes it is so difficult for me to listen — help me I pray. Clarify my life with Your truth, declare Your Word through my life as well. I love going to worship — please help me see You and hear from You each time I attend. I long for Your presence and Your Word to pervade my life. You are my soul's sincere desire. In Jesus' Name, I pray, Amen.

Day 32

A Laser-Guided Life

"The Spirit of the Lord is on me,
because he has anointed me to preach good news to the poor.

He has sent me to proclaim freedom for the prisoners and
recovery of sight for the blind,
to release the oppressed, to proclaim the year of the Lord's favor."

Then he rolled up the scroll, gave it back to the attendant
and sat down. The eyes of everyone in the synagogue were fastened on
him, and he began by saying to them, "Today this scripture is
fulfilled in your hearing."
Luke 4:18-21

Laser guidance is used by the military to direct a missile to a target. A laser beam is aimed at the objective, and the laser's radiation bounces off the target scattering in all directions. This technique is called *painting the target.*

Then the missile launches in the general direction of the target. When it is close enough to detect the reflected energy, the laser seeker focuses on the painted objective and adjusts the projectile trajectory toward the goal. The missile then zeroes in precisely to its target accomplishing its mission. In our passage today Christ inaugurates His ministry among people guided by the laser-focus of God's Word.

The Holy Spirit leads Christ with the focus of the sevenfold directive detailed in today's passage. This represents the third discipline necessary for victorious Christian living – knowing who you are and what you are doing. Mark Twain said, *the two most important days in your life are the day you are born, and the day you find out why.* Jesus knew why He was born and so can we.

Seven phrases define the mission of Jesus, and it is by these statements we are also empowered. His target is you and His Spirit-powered grace is heading your way. Christ is the ideal Man, who provides everything you need to live successfully.

The first guidepost of Jesus' mission is His identification with the Holy Spirit - *the Spirit of the Lord is on me.* Jesus relied first on God's Spirit. Everything in His life flowed from that partnership.

The second signpost of Christ's commission was the phrase; *He has anointed me.* The word *anointed* is special in this context. It directly refers to the Messiah in traditional Jewish thinking. *Christ* means *Messiah,* or, *Anointed One.* It was the designation of His office or His job. Our Savior is equipped and anointed by the Spirit with certain abilities to help us – that's His vocation.

The Old Testament Hebrew word for Messiah is *mashah;* which translates as *Christ* in the New Testament. *Mashah* first referred to the ritual pouring of oil over an individual to set him apart for a special office. Kings, priests, and prophets were all anointed in this way. In our passage, the anointing of the Spirit of

God upon Christ speaks of His unique purpose and commissioning.

The Spirit anoints Jesus to *Preach good news to the poor.* Jesus proclaims His message to all people regardless of financial or social standing.

There was once a little nun from the isolated country of Albania. She felt this compelling burden for the sick people dying on the streets of Calcutta. She moved there and ministered to diseased, dying Hindus by holding them in her arms as they passed from this life. She saw in their faces the form of Christ. In this way, Mother Teresa preached *good news to the poor* without ever saying a word.

Honored with a Nobel Peace Prize, Mother Theresa traveled around the world as an ambassador for the poor. She later said *we think sometimes that poverty is only being hungry, naked and homeless. The poverty of being unwanted, unloved and uncared for is the greatest poverty. We must start in our own homes to remedy this kind of poverty.*[7]

Christ goes on in this passage describing the fourth aspect of His mission - *He has sent me to proclaim freedom for the prisoners.* Since Jesus did not lead a prison-break, we can presume that He meant this phrase in a broader sense. How about men and women who have been imprisoned by habits and desires - those who are less able to choose the right when tempted? How about those who are overwhelmed with lust, or pride or lying? How about those who serve the substitute god Mammon and are seduced by her luxuries? How about physical addiction to alcohol or opiates, to

---

[7] Mother Teresa. (n.d.). BrainyQuote.com. Retrieved February 25, 2016, from BrainyQuote.com Web site: http://www.brainyquote.com/quotes/quotes/m/mothertere130839.html

prescription medications or even nicotine? Jesus liberates those who are bound if we will listen to Him and respond in faith.

The fifth element of Jesus' commission was to bring *recovery of sight to the blind.* Jesus Himself healed the physically blind (John 9:1-7) and then used this miracle to point out the irony of spiritual blindness (9:39-41). In the Gospel of John especially, we see him moving from physical bread to spiritual bread (John 6), from physical water to spiritual water (John 4). So, I think it's possible that Jesus intended the Scripture from Isaiah to include both healings of physical blindness and spiritual blindness. Christ wants to bring light to the dark places of our lives.

The sixth phrase of Christ's self-definition, *to release the oppressed,* stirs a deep sense of mystery in me. Jesus liberates people from the oppression of demonic spirits. He came to destroy the works of the devil - this shouts the question, *who are the oppressed today and how do we minister to them?*

The Greek verb translated here as *release* is *thrauō,* which means - *break into pieces.* In my words, the phrase reads, *to break away the ties of those who are bound.* I think Jesus came to bring justice to those bound by every form of slavery and injustice. The Lord intends to set free the emotionally depleted and damaged. Christ wants to deliver those bound by any form of mental illness or bad habit. Hallelujah!

Jesus reads the seventh expression of His mission statement, *to proclaim the year of the Lord's favor.* He thereby announces the most audacious declaration imaginable, for it was not the literal year of Jubilee celebrated every fifty years in the Hebrew calendar – known commonly as the *year of the Lord's favor.* So, what was He saying?

EVERY DAY JESUS

The Old Testament laws, feasts, and rituals were meant as guideposts leading to God's favor, or blessings. The Jews came to revere those rituals more than God. Jesus preached before His hometown brethren declaring from Isaiah the Prophet the *meaning* of Jubilee. The *Year of Jubilee* was not simply a financial arrangement – it is an opportunity to minister to the poor, bound and afflicted. More pointedly, it is the declaration of God's literal favor upon humanity. Jesus stood before them the physical and spiritual embodiment of God's favor - and they missed it.

What does *the year of the Lord's favor* mean for us? The sin, guilt, and shame that encumbered us is erased, deleted, and canceled. The Lord of Jubilee paid our debt. The life experiences that polluted the image of God in us are now powerless. Jesus comes to restore God's image in us.

Our hearts may condemn us, but Jesus declares that our debt is paid, and we are free because HE IS the year of the Lord's favor. Christ is Jubilee!

My God, I am Your child, help me to live this day for You. I seek You today asking that You would show me the reason I was born – what is my mission O God?

May I walk in the freedom Christ purchased for me and may I proclaim the year of Your favor wherever I go. Help me tell people that You are not mad at them, that You have great grace in store for us through Jesus. Lord, I ask that You empower me by

Your Spirit to live in health, peace, and freedom today. In Jesus' Name, I pray, Amen.

Day 33

The Unseen Audience

All spoke well of him and were amazed at the gracious words that came from his lips. "Isn't this Joseph's son?" they asked.

Jesus said to them, "Surely you will quote this proverb to me: 'Physician, heal yourself! Do here in your hometown what we have heard that you did in Capernaum."

"I tell you the truth," he continued, "no prophet is accepted in his hometown. I assure you that there were many widows in Israel in Elijah's time, when the sky was shut for three and a half years and there was a severe famine throughout the land. Yet Elijah was not sent to any of them, but to a widow in Zarephath in the region of Sidon. And there were many in Israel with leprosy in the time of Elisha the prophet, yet not one of them was cleansed - only Naaman the Syrian."

All the people in the synagogue were furious when they heard this. They got up, drove him out of the town, and took him to the brow of the hill on which the town was built, in order to throw him down the cliff. But he walked right through the crowd and went on his way.

Luke 4:22-30

In Luke 4 we see Jesus coming home to Nazareth with great fanfare, yet his family and neighbors become the first to reject Him. If anyone would have compassion for the rejection we face it is Christ.

I have fought feelings of rejection my whole life. My dad left our home when I was five years old, and I thought it was because of me. Most people have experienced similar feelings sometime during their life. Rejection is a devastating human emotion, and even Jesus experienced it. Christ is the most rejected man in history – while some accept His offer on the cross, multitudes reject Him and turn away in unbelief.

Jesus is fully a man capable of great inner pain. John 1:11-12 describes Christ's situation, *He came to that which was his own,* (family, friends, neighbors) *but his own did not receive him.* Even Christ's family did not understand Him.

Far too many of us experience the pain of rejection that leads to loneliness, low self-esteem, anger, and depression. The Lord feels our ache. Too many people find their identity in their dysfunction. You must choose to ground your identity in Jesus – you are who God says you are – His child.

Psychologist Abraham Maslow suggests rejection is emotionally painful because of our social nature. Our need for love and *belongingness* is a fundamental human motivation. Author John Powell concurs, *Human beings, like plants, grow in the soil of acceptance, not in the atmosphere of rejection.*

How does Jesus handle rejection? He walks away from it. He moves on. In the remainder of Luke 4, He heals, touches and ministers to those who would receive His unconditional love and acceptance. Christ leaves the rejecters behind and pours His unconditional acceptance upon all who came to Him.

What made those people in Nazareth so angry with the Lord that they wanted to throw Him off a cliff? Christ declared that He was the fulfillment of Isaiah's prophecy, and it perplexed them.

This proclamation is bold but is not what infuriated them. Jesus countered their doubts with two stories about Gentiles who received the help of God. Elijah provided the needs of the widow of Sidon and Elisha healed Naaman, the Syrian leper. The Jews were so sure they alone were God's people that they utterly despised other peoples. Bible Scholar William Barclay says *They believed that God created the Gentiles to be fuel for the fires of hell.* Yet, Jesus comes preaching that God looks with favor upon Jews *and Gentiles.*

Luke is writing to unseen spectators. His audience is in churches scattered throughout Syria and the Roman Empire. They must have stood up and cheered as this section of Luke's Gospel was read. God still loves the Jews, but the revelation in this passage is that God loves us - all of us. Though Jesus suffered rejection in His hometown, His examples of grace toward outsiders would scream acceptance to every nation, tongue, and tribe throughout the ages. We are no longer foreigners, but we are now citizens of the kingdom of God. Christ accepts us as His dearly beloved.

I doubt there is a person alive who has not experienced rejection. Country singer Taylor Swift says so whimsically; *You have people come into your life shockingly and surprisingly. You have losses that you never thought you'd experience. You have rejection and you have to learn how to deal with that and how to get up the next day and go on.*

Charles Stanley challenges believers from a Christian perspective; *Too many Christians have a commitment of convenience. They'll stay faithful as long as it's safe and doesn't involve risk, rejection or criticism. Instead of standing alone in the face of challenge or temptation, they check to see which way their friends are going.*

Christians will suffer persecution. In today's culture that usually takes the form of criticism and rejection.

What is your cross to bear? It probably involves risk, refusal, or rebuff. Jesus may have been the most rejected man in history as He hung on a cross for humanity even as He offers us unconditional love. Christ opens His arms with loving acceptance to all who feel the pangs of rejection. Will we do the same? Will we live faithful to the gospel even if it causes rejection?

Dear Lord, I lay my past at Your feet; I submit the shame I feel in the face of rejection and accusation. I give it all to You. I ask for the quality of faith that will stand strong in the face of overwhelming rejection. Your way is the path to complete joy, peace and hope. I pray for the strength Christ has as He moves forward and beyond the rejection of His family and neighbors. In Your Name, I pray, Amen.

Day 34

The Creative Word of Jesus

Then he went down to Capernaum, a town in Galilee, and on the Sabbath began to teach the people. They were amazed at his teaching, because his message had authority.

In the synagogue there was a man possessed by a demon, an evil spirit. He cried out at the top of his voice, "Ha! What do you want with us, Jesus of Nazareth? Have you come to destroy us? I know who you are - the Holy One of God!"

"Be quiet!" Jesus said sternly. "Come out of him!" Then the demon threw the man down before them all and came out without injuring him.

All the people were amazed and said to each other, "What is this teaching? With authority and power he gives orders to evil spirits and they come out!" And the news about him spread throughout the surrounding area.

Jesus left the synagogue and went to the home of Simon. Now Simon's mother-in-law was suffering from a high fever, and they asked Jesus to help her. So he bent over her and rebuked the

fever, and it left her. She got up at once and began to wait on them.
Luke 4:31-39

God the Son spoke the worlds into existence, and He still speaks to us. Christ roared, and stars raced into space sprinkling the universe with a zillion prisms of light.

Dr. Luke is building a case in his gospel – a case for the sovereignty of Christ in personal affairs. In the context of Luke 4:1-13 we are given a ringside seat to observe Christ battling the prince of temptation in the wilderness. Jesus is victorious in His battle against Satan, and He returns to Nazareth in the power of the Holy Spirit. The Lord then initiates His public ministry on earth by declaring His personal mission statement, *The Spirit of the Lord is upon me...to preach good news...proclaim freedom...recovery of sight and proclaim the year of the Lord's favor.* When His hometown of Nazareth rejects Him, Christ moves on to Capernaum where He promptly evicts a demonic presence. The people are amazed at the authority with which He speaks – His ministry is rolling full speed ahead. From this point forward Jesus' life has only two speeds – fast and faster.

In our passage today we find Jesus arriving at the home of Peter's feverish mother, who is suffering. He utters the word of healing, and her fever flees. What kind of man does that? A man who personally loves every individual! What would the Lord speak to you today?

Christ is not just a personal savior – He is also a healer. Jesus verbally *rebukes the fever*, it obeys and leaves. What do you say when you speak to a fever? He spoke to an inanimate object, and it obeyed His voice similar to when He spoke into the darkness and it became light at creation.

Hebrews 1:1-3 illuminates Jesus' behavior from another vantage point, *In the past God spoke to our forefathers through the prophets at many times and in various ways, but in these last days he has spoken to us by his Son, whom he appointed heir of all things, and through whom he made the universe. The Son is the radiance of God's glory and the exact representation of his being, sustaining all things by his powerful word.* In Luke, Christ heals Peter's mother by the power of His Word. We are witnessing the same Lord who created the cosmos exercising His authority to personally help people. His Word has power!

Imagine what Jesus could do in your life by the authority of His Word! Whom would He heal? What would He rebuke? What would He command to go? Negativity, hidden addiction, fear, doubt, lust, murmuring, pride – all commanded to go!

Every Sunday there are men and women of God standing in pulpits all over the world preaching God's Word. Christ will breathe new life into your soul if you apply faith to that preaching. Somewhere in your house is a Bible that contains a living Word for you. Books, radio, television, CDs, DVDs, and the internet can all relay God's Word if you look and listen in the right places. All it takes is a listening ear and a believing heart.

My wife loves her clunky old-fashioned radio. It has a round dial that tunes in various stations. To listen to a program without static, you must hold the antennae, stand on one foot while dangling your left hand in the air as if you were an antennae extension. Then slowly turn the knob with your right hand until you reach a station with clarity. Listening to God's Word is often like that old radio. You must incline your heart with great sensitivity to hear God's Voice speaking to your innermost being.

Cultivating the inner awareness of God's Word and Spirit is central to the Christian life. Living in obedience to the Voice of Jesus gives you authority, clarity, and significance. Do you really want to hear God's voice and feel His healing touch? Commit yourself to opening your Bible daily. Then pause and listen. I challenge you to pause for seven minutes of silence. Tune out all the noise and just listen. Turn off your mind, your thoughts and agenda to sit before God. He's wired you for more than you can imagine – to hear the song of the ages and to see the Glory of God. He created you to know HIS voice.

Dear Lord Jesus, I ask You to speak Your Word of life into my soul. I believe that You speak the word of healing into my soul today as You did to Peter's mother-in-law and as You did when You created the worlds. May Your goodness and grace continue to flow through me to the world.
In Your Name, I pray, Amen.

Day 35

Super-Sized Healing

When the sun was setting, the people brought to Jesus all
who had various kinds of sickness, and laying his hands on each
one, he healed them. Moreover, demons came out of many people,
shouting, "You are the Son of God!" But he rebuked them and
would not allow them to speak,
because they knew he was the Christ.
Luke 4:40-41

My older brother Bob was always a big guy, and children often called him mean names like *Fatty*, *Fatso* and *blubber-butt*. Later, due to his service in the Vietnam War, Bob had terrible nightmares. He tried to silence those memories and dreams with toxic portions of food, alcohol and pot.

Eventually, Bob grew to weigh over 500 pounds. Desperately trying to change his life, Bob decided to have surgery to remove a large portion of his stomach. He died of surgical complications at only 50 years of age.

In the big picture, my brother was an unhappy person. His size prevented him from engaging in normal life activities. Bob had a hard time loving himself for who he was, and this led to cycles of depression comforted only by more eating and drinking. I mourn the loss of my brother and the unhappiness he felt most of his life. Bob needed the super-sized healing that only Jesus can give.

In Jen Larsen's new book, *Stranger Here: How Weight-Loss Surgery Transformed My Body and Messed with My Head*, she explains how losing 180 pounds wasn't all she thought it would be. Her fiercely honest writing moved me. While it is not a spiritual read, it is compelling for anyone who is struggling with weight issues or knows someone who is drowning in the murky waters of an eating disorder.

Many people suffer today from weight problems, a bad self-image, and self-loathing. People are suffering, and not just overweight people. I remember a movie star in the eighties named Farrah Fawcett, many considered her to be the most beautiful woman in the world. She said in an interview with Barbara Walters that when she looked into the mirror she only saw an ugly girl - then she cried.

Larsen says in her book, *I thought that my body was wrong when I was obese; I thought my body was wrong when I was thin past the point of health. I thought there was something wrong with my body whatever I looked like because there's always just one more thing to fix before I look perfect...I felt helpless before. I tried to dodge out of the feeling by getting weight loss surgery, and now I'm angry, that I wasn't fixed, yes. But also that so many people deal with this, this exact and pervasive struggle at whatever size they are, whatever shape, whatever they do. There is no perfect weight or size.*

I believe Jesus wants to touch people like my brother Bob, Farrah Fawcett and Jen Larsen at the core of their being. He can give super-sized healing and self-acceptance like no other.

Luke 4:40 above describes *how* Jesus *healed* people, and Doctor Luke uses the specific Greek word *therapeuo* to define

Christ's healing gift. This word means, *to wait upon menially.* It gives the sense of a nurse applying a therapy that brings soothing comfort from pain. Jesus administers therapeutic healing, massage-like therapy to the body and soul.

Contemporary Christian music artists *Mercy Me* sing in their song *Beautiful, You're beautiful, you are made for so much more than all of this. You're beautiful! You are treasured, you are sacred, you are His. You're Beautiful!* May the Lord use us to love people who are suffering from the deceptions of our culture and a skewed self-image.

You are indescribably precious in God's eyes, crafted in your mother's womb by the hand of the Almighty. You are an amazing reflection of the Most High God, made in His image and destined to live forever in the light of His glory. Allow Jesus to speak the word of healing to your heart, soul and body.

Lord Jesus, I pray today that You will open my eyes to see myself as You created me to be — well and whole. I pray that Your healing presence will fill my heart, body, and soul. May You use me today to impart Your healing power, grace and peace to all those I meet. In Your Name, I pray, Amen.

DAVE HOLLAND

Day 36

Out from the Lonely Place

At daybreak Jesus went out to a solitary place. The people were looking for him and when they came to where he was, they tried to keep him from leaving them. But he said, "I must preach the good news of the kingdom of God to the other towns also, because that is why I was sent." And he kept on preaching in the synagogues of Judea.
Luke 4:42-44

Most people run from the lonely place – Jesus sought it. Obsessed with the desire for *friends* we spend day and night on *Facebook, Twitter,* and cell phones, hoping that somebody will care about us. *Friending* people we barely know, we crave people who will make us feel like we matter.

Loneliness is a terrible feeling, and we will pay almost any price to avoid it. I have observed families at food pantries without enough money for food, yet they have five smartphones among them with unlimited data plans. I submit that cell phones and social media will not satisfy the craving of the human heart for real love.

The great French scientist, Blaise Pascal, says in his book *Pensees, All humanity's problems stem from man's inability to sit quietly in a room alone.*

Jesus shows us another path, one that will lead to ultimate fulfillment. Christ feeds His interior person by going to a *solitary place*. The Greek word Luke employs is *eremos* meaning *desolate, lonesome, desert*. The Lord sought an unsocial place to be alone with God. Something very significant happens there in the early morning hour.

The Son of God received His marching orders for the day in the stillness of the dawn. In those times, God revealed to Jesus where He was going, what He was doing, and much of what He would say. A moment in the morning with God makes for a day of significance.

I remember reading about a Russian Rabbi who was sent to a gulag in Siberia. Early in the morning chill, before the work camp began to stir, he would walk the perimeter of the grounds and pray. One morning a guard on patrol saw him and shouted at him with a staccato, machine-gun-like voice, *Stop! Where are you going? What are you doing? Who do you think you are?*

Young man, the old rabbi replied, *I will pay you a year's wage if you ask me those questions every day.* The rabbi understood that the direction of our life boils down to our responses to these simple questions.

Jesus received answers to these questions in His quiet place with God. From there He set out like a man on fire with a mission. He knew His purpose, *I must preach the good news of the kingdom of God to the other towns also, because that is why I was sent.*

I believe every person has a purpose, a reason for being, a mission to fulfill. Until we understand who we are in God's eyes and what we are meant to do with our lives, we will wander aimlessly like a boat cast adrift in the fog.

EVERY DAY JESUS

Jesus shows us the pathway to peace by His simple example – a model that would bring peace to millions of people.

The Anxiety and Depression Association of America (ADAA) is a leader in education, training, and research for anxiety, *Obsessive-Compulsive Disorder, Post-Traumatic Stress Disorder,* depression, and related ailments. They say that anxiety disorders are the most common mental illness in the U.S., affecting over 40 million adults. So many people are suffering from anxiety and depression! This disease impacts almost every family in America.

I submit to you that a moment in the presence of God not only relieves but heals this plague. Medication, social media, mass media, and unprecedented levels of human communications cannot fill the place in the human heart designed for God.

Pastor and author, Ron Mehl, once said to me that he felt loneliness was the heart's cry for God. God will transform our lives if we learn to interpret this seemingly negative emotion as God calling us to a quiet place with Him.

Jesus met with God early in the morning, and it anchored His soul through some of the worst human sufferings in history. Christ shows us the way to peace with God, peace with people, and peace with ourselves - a way that begins in a quiet place alone with God.

Aloneness is really just an illusion – there is nowhere you can go to escape the presence of God. God knows your deepest thoughts and Jesus feels your innermost longings as He is in us and with us and for us. Every moment you spend seeking an awareness of His presence brings you closer to the meaning and purpose of your life.

Ground me in your peace Lord Jesus. Lead me to that quiet, place of prayer at the Father's feet each morning. Give me a sensitivity to the leading of the Holy Spirit and help me discern His direction for each day. I want You — Jesus - in my life every day. Draw me to the quiet place with You - conquer my loneliness, worries, and busyness with Your Presence. May I drink daily from the well of Your living water. In the Father's Name, I pray, Amen.

Day 37

Living on Purpose

But he said, "I must preach the good news of the kingdom of God to the other towns also, because that is why I was sent." And he kept on preaching in the synagogues of Judea.
Luke 4:43-44

The person living an arbitrary life creates his own hell. It's like living on the bottom of the ocean where everything creeps in darkness, and void of any light. You swim from one tiresome obligation to the next, until you finally lay your bones down to sleep permanently. Real life – joy-filled, obstacle shattering, hell-be-damned life - begins when your faith in God defines your purpose for living. Jesus lived on point, on purpose.

Summarizing where we have been in this devotional journey, we see that first Luke lays down both a scriptural and supernatural foundation for God's Son to enter the world. Born to the sound of angelic choirs, Mary's Song, and simple shepherds singing, Christ arrives according to plan. God was not surprised when you were born either – He has a strategy for your life as well. You are a part of His eternal plan.

Prophetic announcements greet Christ's arrival at the temple as Anna, Simeon, and the Temple scholars marvel at the Child would-be Messiah. But it was that gravelly voice in the wilderness of John the Baptist, which brought divine definition to Christ's destiny; *Behold the Lamb of God!* He cried out. How could John possibly know his cousin Jesus was the sacrifice for the world?

John saw more in a moment than most of us see in a lifetime. Jesus, the Lamb of God upon whom the Spirit rests, would change the direction of the cosmos. The Holy Spirit then propels Christ from the baptismal waters down a desert path toward His sacrificial future.

Have you ever left church feeling warm in your soul only to find great difficulties waiting for you? Jesus knows that sensation. The Spirit drives Jesus forward by leading Him to a wilderness boxing battle with the Devil. Christ defeats Satan with the sword of the Spirit and the Word of God - you can too.

The see-saw cosmic battle continues with rejection in His hometown of Nazareth and then His acceptance in Capernaum. Devils try to divert Jesus. The crowds pull at His clothes clamoring for His attention. Unwavering in His desire to follow God's direction, Jesus leaves the burgeoning crowds to pray. From the place of prayer, Christ steams forward like a locomotive rolling down the tracks toward the most fruitful period of His ministry in Capernaum, Judea, and Samaria.

Jesus will not deviate from God's plan.

Luke paints the picture of a man on fire with a mission in this opening section of his gospel. Determined, directed and driving toward the fulfillment of His human existence, Christ shares His life with God's people along the way.

I read once that a man will never feel fulfilled until he finds the work and reason for which he was born. Only God brings us to such clarity concerning His will for our lives.

In the mid-'70s, I buried myself in Bible College studies and occasionally surfaced to visit my mother and Aunt Gerri. Mom had been drinking heavily that afternoon, and she began to slur loudly, *I always knew you were called to the ministry, God always had His hand on your life.*

I was confused by her words as I thought I was the first active Christian in our family. Aunt Gerri, who was sober, filled in the back-story.

While my mother was pregnant with me, she and my father were Christians but not getting along. There was a woman in their small house church who many believed had divine insight - She also had eyes for my dad. The supposed prophetess declared that my mother and the baby she carried were evil.

My father believed the errant prophecy and shunned mom for the rest of her pregnancy. She was so distraught that the doctor told Mom if she didn't change her emotional state she could lose her baby. Desperate, my mother called out to God and dedicated her baby to His service if the Lord would spare him. Mom named me *David* to honor that promise.

My parents later divorced and strayed from their faith. Mom experienced many life-choking events, and she turned to alcohol for relief. During my early teen years, our home was drowning in depression and alcoholism. Then, God called my number.

I was sixteen years old when God sovereignly called me back to Himself. I received forgiveness for my sins by putting my faith in Christ, and in Him I found my purpose for living. While life has not been all sunshine and moonbeams, I thank the Lord Jesus for the overflowing life He has given me.

This first section of Luke's Gospel concludes with the ongoing activity of Christ's life - *He kept on preaching*. Luke shows us how to live like Jesus every day – continuing in His work despite the obstacles and distractions along the way. Not just on the good days but also on the ordinary days. Christ demonstrates that living on purpose holds the potential for both conflict and peace.

What were you born to do? Why were you born? Paul said in Ephesians 4:1, *I urge you to live a life worthy of the calling you have received.*

Too often we are plagued by our biggest mistakes - *I can't do that because I've done this*…But God does not eliminate us by our failures. God defines us by His greatest triumph – raising Christ from the dead through the power of the Holy Spirit. Jesus includes us in His resurrection victory parade.

In the brightest and darkest moments of your life, your calling to serve God is your anchor. Father God loves you and calls you to honor Him every day. He does not cast you aside after you let Him down. Instead, He is slowly teaching you to live like Jesus every day. Rise up to that high calling.

Like Christ, you must go forward sharing God's love in conversation, in spontaneous acts of kindness and deliberate demonstrations of God's mercy. It is the purpose for which Christ saves you and me. Every day is the day of salvation when serving God is your purpose for living.

Lord Jesus, thank You for Your Word that leads me into Your lifestyle every day. Strengthen me to walk like You into my God-prepared destiny. Touch me with Your power and lead me with Your grace for I am Yours. O Lord, I am Yours every day. Amen.

DAVE HOLLAND

Day 38

Fishing with a Carpenter

One day as Jesus was standing by the Lake
of Gennesaret, with the people crowding around him
and listening to the word of God, he saw at the
water's edge two boats, left there by the fishermen,
who were washing their nets. He got into one of the
boats, the one belonging to Simon, and asked him to
put out a little from shore. Then he sat down and
taught the people from the boat.

When he had finished speaking, he said to
Simon, "Put out into deep water, and let down the
nets for a catch."

Simon answered, "Master, we've worked
hard all night and haven't caught anything. But
because you say so, I will let down the nets."

When they had done so, they caught such a
large number of fish that their nets began to break.
Luke 5:1-6

Ever had a hard day at work and all you can think of is getting home? You finally walk through the door of your house and you can think of nothing more than getting into something comfortable, sitting in your favorite chair and relaxing. Jesus calls at such a time as this.

Luke invites us to see Christ as He speaks to us in our vulnerable moments. He beckons us when it is not convenient, and His love often demands sacrifice. The Lord is teaching multitudes of people who crowd in close to hear Him preach when He suddenly conscripts Peter and his boat to use as a makeshift pulpit. Thus begins the call of the disciples and thus begins our call to follow Jesus.

Peter and the boys were tired and frustrated at their failure to catch fish. They were deep inside their heads when the Rabbi asked to use their boat. Amid their weariness, Jesus says cheerily, "let's go fish!" Imagine a Carpenter turned Rabbi telling them the fishermen to fish where they had just failed.

Jesus doesn't ask Peter whether he *feels* like casting nets for fish. So, Peter explains to Jesus that they have been fishing all night and hadn't caught a thing, "No fish biting today Jesus, come back another time," he seems to say.

Isn't that the way we respond when the Lord calls us? "Yes Lord, but I had a long day," or "You don't understand how busy I've been Lord." Too often when Jesus comes to get into the boat of our life, we have excuses for Him. Are we ready to be obedient no matter how we feel?

It took about 2 seconds for Peter to come out with his next response though, "BUT, if you say so, we'll try again." I'm sure Peter wanted to know how they were possibly going to catch fish in the middle of the day. Yet, he chooses to obey. Peter and the fishermen soon see the miracle of a huge catch. Doing what God asks doesn't always make sense, and it's not always logical, but it is always successful. The fishermen go where Jesus instructs and cast their nets in the water - again. Their nets come up bursting with fish!

Obedience requires determination. Many priorities will tug for your attention, but you must decide to focus on Jesus. Trust that following His direction will be the most effective, important, and wisest decision you can make. The disciples learned that it wasn't about their logic, nets, or ability to fish - it was all about Jesus. Will you determine to listen to Jesus and cast your nets again?

There is a healing balm in Jesus' words, "Come to me, all you who are weary and burdened, and I will give you rest. (Matthew 11:28) The Lord understands the everyday grind of life and bids us come to Him with our fatigue.

Writer Anais Nin looks at weariness from another perspective, *Love never dies a natural death. It dies because we don't know how to replenish its source. It dies of blindness and errors and betrayals. It dies of illness and wounds; it dies of weariness, of witherings, of tarnishings.* Replenishing the source of our love for God and refueling the desire to serve Him will come from the Lord but we must come to Him and receive a fresh word.

Paul relates in Galatians 6:9. *Let us not become weary in doing good, for at the proper time we will reap a harvest if we do not give up.* Peter obeyed the Lord's call and went home that night with more than fish to show for his efforts. There's a boatload of fish out there in the sea of humanity, it's time to go fish – let the miracle begin.

Jesus, do you really want to get into my boat? Use my talents or assets? You can if you want to but I'm really tired. Nevertheless, I choose today to do what You ask me to do. Strengthen me when I can't see the harvest, prepare me for the day of fruitfulness You have planned. Yes, Lord, I will go where You want me to go and do what You want me to do. Amen

Day 39

The Leper's Story

While Jesus was in one of the towns, a man came along who was covered with leprosy. When he saw Jesus, he fell with his face to the ground and begged him, "Lord, if you are willing, you can make me clean."

Jesus reached out his hand and touched the man. "I am willing," he said. "Be clean!" And immediately the leprosy left him.

Then Jesus ordered him, "Don't tell anyone, but go, show yourself to the priest and offer the sacrifices that Moses commanded for your cleansing, as a testimony to them."
Luke 5:12-15

My name isn't important, *Leper*, is the only name you will ever know.

It all started one day as I was getting ready for work. I noticed a small discolored patch on my right arm. Slowly, it grew larger. I knew the Law of Moses said any blemish like this had to be examined by the priest. If the spot were leprosy, I would lose everything. I was so scared I hid it for a while. Eventually, the spot grew and I had to go to the priest for an examination. My worst nightmare came true. He called it leprosy and judged me unclean.

Leprosy is worse than death – it's slow torture. Banished from God's presence, I could not legally worship in the Temple. Forbidden to associate with my family and friends, I grew so lonely. I had to live in a camp outside the village. Walking the streets begging, I would have to call out, *Unclean, unclean* to all who came near me. The humiliations of these words stick to me like moldy syrup. I shouted out to everyone that I was cursed and unclean. Crowds parted as I drew near. The children mocked my cry of *unclean*, laughed at me and threw stones at me.

That's not the worst part - I was untouchable- no one would dare touch me or they would be judged unclean as well. Can you imagine the pain of going untouched by human hands, never feeling the warmth of family and never clasping the hands of friends?

I longed to be wanted and needed. I yearned to have friends and a family of my own. I ached to have a name. I was simply the *Leper* – until Jesus came along.

People said this man Jesus comes from God, a great prophet like Elijah. He went around the area healing people and teaching them. I heard that He had healed the lame and cured the blind. I had even heard that lepers like me were cleansed. I went to see Him, and His teaching was more powerful than you can imagine. When I saw Him, I knew that He was the answer to all my problems, but I couldn't get to Him. He taught the crowd and then He left.

EVERY DAY JESUS

The day came when I heard the noise of the crowd in the streets ahead of me. Someone cried out the name *Jesus*. HE's coming toward our town.

I ran in the direction of the crowd, *Unclean*, I cried, *Unclean*. I am not sure how it happened but the next thing I knew the Rabbi was standing right in front of me.

I did the only thing I knew to do. I fell on my face in front of Jesus. I was ashamed to speak to Him as I was dirty and disfigured - a grotesque parody of a man. I could hardly find the voice to speak, but I cried, *Lord, If you are willing, you can make me clean*. I closed my eyes. I guess I expected Him to treat me like everyone else did - walking away disgusted. I knew He could heal me – but I didn't dare hope that He would. I could hear the jeers of the crowd and feel the revulsion of the people standing near me. I will never forget what Jesus did next.

He touched me! I couldn't believe it at first, HE touched me. I remember the warmth of His hand- the gentle clutch of His fingers on my arm. I looked up from the ground and my eyes met His. There was no disgust, no loathing, no fear – only love.

Christ spoke with the sonic boom of a thousand thunderbolts, *I am willing, be cleansed*. At first, I didn't notice anything until I looked at my hands- the sores were gone- the two fingers I had lost were back on my hand. Slowly, I took the clothes away from my arms, and instead of festering flesh, I saw my arms restored. He cleansed every spot from my skin. On the ground before Him, I praised God with tears of joy. Then, Jesus lifted me to my feet.

You should have seen the crowds that followed Him after that. They came from all over the countryside bringing sick people to see the Master. But controversy seemed to follow Him as closely as the crowds. Were the leaders in Jerusalem jealous of His power or popularity?

It was only a short time later I heard that the Jesus who touched me had been killed in Jerusalem. Crucified, can you imagine? He took away my despicable disease and crushing isolation only to die alone and suffering on a cross. I wept uncontrollably.

Later, I met His disciples and they told me the good news. Jesus isn't dead - God raised Him from the dead - He's alive! It was easy for me to believe – He had already raised me from virtual death.

Today I follow the Living Lord - I serve the one who set me free from leprosy and sin. Now people read about me and some of you are no different than I was.

Sometimes you feel like an outcast and untouchable - you feel violated, guilty and unclean. Loneliness haunts you, and the sense of isolation makes you want to give up. I want to tell you that Jesus cares - He wants to touch you just like He touched me. He will pick you up off the ground and set you on your feet again. Jesus will heal you and empower you to live for Him.

Some of you are unclean - you have leprosy in your soul. Maybe not on your skin but you have leprosy of the heart - the heartache of a hundred different varieties is eating away at you. If you call on Jesus today, He will wash your leprous heart clean and make you whole again. He is *willing* to heal you and make you whole. He wants to be the miracle worker in your life.

Lord Jesus, I have leprosy of the soul. Help me, heal me of this scourge that plagues my conscience. I too often hide from You, as if You don't know the things that I think and say and do. I hear the message of the leper today — You are willing to make me clean — help my unbelief. I choose today to put my hope in You and trust that you are working out my healing and restoration. I pray in Your name, Amen.

DAVE HOLLAND

Day 40

Sharing the Power of His Indestructible Life

Yet the news about him spread all the more,
so that crowds of people came to hear him and
to be healed of their sicknesses. But Jesus often
withdrew to lonely places and prayed.
Luke 5:16

This King-Priest did not arise because of a
genealogical right under the law to be a priest, but by
the power of an indestructible life.
Hebrews 7:16, TPT

The journey in Christ's life and the Gospel of Luke begins. The preparations are made, and Jesus now turns His Face toward Jerusalem. His ministry takes on huge proportions as he nears the population center of Israel. His miracles also grow in great numbers. Jesus moves to the center of Jewish life and religion, and the conflict also grows exponentially. During this next phase of Jesus' life, we see the Master in His prime ministry years. His greatest miracles are counter-balanced with constant harassment from His critics. Are you ready to experience the joys and sorrows of this next period of His life? To walk through it with Him?

DAVE HOLLAND

What will you do with the rest of your life? The above verses summarize the first chapters of Christ's life from His birth to the calling of the disciples. What verse will summarize your life when you lay your bones down at the end of it all? Are you participating in the power of His indestructible life?

Jesus has a purpose for you and me - we need Him – our destiny links with His. But the question remains, *Will we willingly walk side by side with Him, grounded in our faith, confidently facing all that lies ahead?*

The first four and a half chapters of Luke lay the foundation of Jesus' life and ministry, and we are invited to build our lives on that same groundwork. From angelic pronouncements to demonic temptations, Jesus comes shining through as the Anointed One. We have walked with Him through Luke's first four chapters of preparation and can live confidently, knowing the Lord is with us every day.

Christ's baptism showed us who Jesus is and His temptations showed us who He is not. Our baptism works in that same fashion – it is planting our flag in the ground and announcing to the world who we are in Christ. Our resistance to temptation tells the Devil that we are not following him. Together these experiences proclaim that we will not turn back from the faith.

I was baptized in 1970 and it launched a new era in my life. Though I was so far from perfect, I knew that I was His and He was mine. I surrendered my destiny into His hands. I remember how disappointed I was that temptation was not washed away as well. Baptism is a one-time event, but resisting temptation is a daily struggle.

EVERY DAY JESUS

Unlike Jesus, I lose many battles with the tempter. I remember trying so hard not to swear. It was a terrible, foul habit that I succumbed to every day and repented of every Sunday in church. Eventually, I gave up and told the Lord I was sorry, but I couldn't stop failing in that area. I surrendered. That's when the Lord started to work. About six months later I realized that swearing was no longer a part of my life, Jesus had quietly, slowly won the victory. All I had to do was let Him fight the battle and trust that He would bring success at the right time. Christ defeats the devil every time. Will you surrender and let Him fight for you?

I suspect that many of you have struggled to do this devotion every day. It's okay, there's no law that says you must. Blessing waits for you every day if you push through, establish the discipline and reap the fruit of God's blessing. We turn now to the next period in Christ's life in Luke 5-9 – the Galilean Ministry period. It is the season of miracles – signs and wonders affirming Jesus as the Messiah. To many, it is the most exciting period in Jesus' life. This could launch the most exhilarating time in your life as well.

The next devotional is called *Extraordinary Jesus*. It travels along as this one has done but it challenges us to a higher level of living. Every miracle of Jesus is an opportunity to believe for greater things.

Luke tells us that the news of Jesus spread everywhere. People talked about Him in the synagogues and the marketplaces. While we might send out news releases, call photographers, create a website and set up a Facebook page – after all, we want to get this show on the road - Jesus simply interacted with people. Jesus was extraordinarily different.

If we walk the roads of Palestine with Him amazing can start to happen again in us. Water still flows from the Rock and the best wine is saved for last. Let's begin our journey to real-life - abundant life with Jesus. We have tried average so now let's try astonishing with our *Extraordinary Jesus* in the next installment of daily devotions in Luke.

Lord Jesus, how I have come to love You. Strengthen me for the next chapter in my life I pray. You have done incredible things in Your life and mine, but I want more. Show me Your glory and the glory of the Father that I might worship you more fully. Let my walk with You grow as your ministry grows in this next phase of my life. Help me to face criticism with grace as you did. I confess my inclination to get angry and defensive when I feel attacked. Help me turn to the Word and the Father during these times. Baptize me today with the Spirit You were baptized in, give me the strength to resist the Tempter as You did. Sharpen my focus on God even in the midst of busyness. I ask that I can share in the power of Your indestructible life.
In Your name, I pray, Amen.

Epilogue

Note to Church Leadership

This devotional will speak to the guys and gals you lead who simply want to know Jesus. Most have not trained in Bible College or Seminary and care little about the nuances of faith we obsess over. It is my prayer that you would use this simple work to teach your people in the ways of Jesus using HIS life as the pattern of discipleship.

I have pastored for over thirty-eight years and I often observed pastors and denominations using starchy prescriptions for new believers. *Read the Bible, pray, go to church, tithe, become faithful members, serve tirelessly, and give to missions...* While these are good convictions, are we inventing a new Christian code? Are we putting yokes of structure and institutionalism on people that make them grow weary? I believe our mandate is larger than that – the scriptures command us to preach Christ and love one another. Many people are tired of Churchianity but are hungry for a relationship with Jesus. This devotional is written to simply feed that hunger.

I came to faith in Christ during the height of the Jesus Movement in 1970 at Angelus Temple, the headquarters Church of the Foursquare Movement. That church exposed me to many great leaders such as Jack Hayford, Paul (David) Yonggi Cho, David du

Plessis, Ron Mehl, Roy Hicks Jr., Jerry Cook, Dr. Guy P. Duffield, Chuck Smith, Josh McDowell, Reinhart Bonnke and Bill Bright. These mentors invested more in my life than I can ever repay.

As an evangelical who graduated *Magna Cum Laude* from Gordon-Conwell Theological Seminary, I'm honored that Billy Graham signed my diploma. I treasure my training. But I once heard Francis Schaeffer say that a true intellectual can put the truth into terms a common person can understand. That is my sole goal here.

My approach to scripture is largely guided by Gordon Fee's work, *How to Read the Bible for All Its Worth*. I pray that this book will reflect his conviction to interpret Bible truths clothed in their original context and applied to modern living.

I am grateful for the blessing of education but I readily identify with Paul's allusion to his education in Philippians 3:4-9, *I consider these great blessings as dung when compared to the surpassing greatness of the knowledge of Christ*. In the end, it's only a relationship with Jesus that matters.

This book is not simply an inspirational devotional like *Our Daily Bread*. Devotionals like that are helpful but very brief. I hope to bring depth and focus on this gospel in the sequence in which it was written. *Every Day Jesus* is designed to walk believers through the life of Christ in Luke's Gospel event by event, paragraph by paragraph. I pray that sound exegesis undergirds each chapter and that the power of Christ's Spirit releases energy to grow in the reader's life.

Every Day Jesus is the first of a series of devotionals gently leading believers through the life of Christ in Luke. I am writing my way completely through this book, verse by verse and I invite you to join me on this Jesus journey.

Pastor, imagine if the believers in your fellowship read and pray their way through the life of Jesus – what kind of Christian will result? I believe they will become strong, stable, balanced, fire-breathing followers of Christ.

More than anything, I pray that the people who read *Everyday Jesus* become like Jesus and that it assists church leaders in the great challenge of teaching people to love like Christ, to walk with Him and to be Jesus to the world.

DAVE HOLLAND

RESOURCES USED FOR *EVERY DAY JESUS*

Aland, Kurt, ed. 1985. *Synopsis of the Four Gospels.* New York: United Bible Societies.

Amoral, Joe. 2011. *Understanding Jesus, Cultural Insights into the Words and Deeds of Christ.* New York, NY: Faith Words.

Anderson, Leith. 2005 *Jesus, An Intimate Portrait of the Man, His Land, and His People.* Minneapolis, MN: Bethany House.

Barclay, William. 1956. *The Gospel of Luke, The Daily Study Bible Series.* Philadelphia, PA: The Westminster Press.

Buckingham, Jamie. 1991. *Parables, Poking Holes in Religious Balloons.* Lake Mary, FL: Creation House.

Childers, Charles L. 1971. *The Gospel According to St. Luke, Beacon Bible Commentary.* Kansas City, Missouri: Beacon Hill Press.

Courson, Jon. 2003. *Application Commentary.* Nashville, TN: Thomas Nelson.

Edersheim, Alfred. 1905. *The Life and Times of Jesus the Messiah.* New York, NY: Longman's, Green, and Co.

Erdman, Charles R. 1975. *The Gospel of Luke.* Philadelphia, PA: The Westminster Press.

France, R.T. 2013. *Luke, Teach the Text Series.* Grand Rapids, MI: Baker Books.

Geldenhuys, Norval. 1983. *The Gospel of Luke, The New International Commentary on the New Testament.* Grand Rapids, MI: Wm. B. Eerdmans Publishing Company.

The Holy Bible: New International Version. 1984. Colorado Springs, Co: International Bible Society.

Hughes, R. Kent. 1998. *Luke, Volume 1, That You May Know the Truth.* Wheaton, IL: Crossway Books.

Jenkins, Jerry B., Lahaye, Tim. 2009. *Luke's Story, by Faith Alone.* New York, NY: Putnam Praise, G.P. Punam's Sons.

Johnson, Luke Timothy. 2011. *Prophetic Jesus, Prophetic Church.* Grand Rapids, MI: William B. Eerdmans Publishing Company.

LaSor, William Sanford. 1961. *Great Personalities of the New Testament, Their Lives and Times.* Westwood, NJ: Fleming H. Revell Company.

Lucado, Max. 2002. *Just Like Jesus, a Thirty Day Walk With the Savior.* Nashville, TN: Thomas Nelson.

Moore, Beth. 2007. *Jesus, 90 Days With the One and Only.* Nashville, TN: B&H Publishing Group.

Morgan, G. Campbell. 1943. The Parables and Metaphors of Our Lord. Old Tappan, NJ: Fleming H. Revell Company.

Morris, Leon. 1974. *Luke, Tyndale New Testament Commentaries.* Grand Rapids, MI: William B. Eerdman's Publishing.

Muggeridge, Malcolm. 1975. *Jesus, The Man Who Lives.* New York, NY: Harper & Row Publishers.

Nouwen, Henri. 2001. *Jesus, A Gospel.* Maryknoll, NY: Orbis Books.

Ogilvie, Lloyd John. 1979. *Autobiography of God, God Revealed in the Parables of Jesus.* Ventura, CA: Regal Books.

Peterson, Eugene H. 1993. *The Message*. Colorado Springs, CO: Navpress.

Renner, Rick. 2003. *Sparkling Gems from the Greek*. Tulsa, OK: Harrison House Publishing.

Stronstad, Roger. 2012. *The Charismatic Theology of St. Luke*. Grand Rapids, MI: Baker Academic.

Trench, R.C. 1977. *Notes on the Parables of Our Lord*. Grand Rapids, MI: Baker Book House.

Wangerin, Walter Jr. 2005. *Jesus, A Novel*. Grand Rapids, MI: Zondervan.

Wieland, Albert Cassel. 1947. A New Harmony of the Gospels. Grand Rapids, Michigan: Wm. B. Eerdmans Publishing Co.

Zodhiates, Spiro. 1990. *The Hebrew-Greek Key Study Bible*. Chattanooga, TN: AMG Publishers.

ABOUT THE AUTHOR

Dave Holland helps people become more like Christ. It is his mission to *Love God and Love People*. He has been serving God as a pastor for over thirty-eight years. He planted a thriving church in Brockton, Massachusetts starting with just sixteen people and from that church, he mothered seven other congregations in Massachusetts. He currently resides in Destin, Florida.

Born in Los Angeles Dave has lived for significant periods of time in the East, Midwest, Colorado and the Southeast. Dave and wife Jonie love their five grown children who are scattered about America and Europe leaving them to scurry about all year trying to see their fourteen grandchildren.

While living in New England, Dave discovered that he bleeds Patriot blue and craves any news concerning his beloved Celtics, Patriots, and Red Sox - once a New Englander always a New Englander. He also plays guitar, reads, and collects books.

Dave attended Life Pacific College graduating in 1979. He was ordained by the Foursquare Movement in 1981. While pastoring in New England, he received his Master of Arts Degree from Gordon-Conwell Theological Seminary graduating *Magnum Cum Laude* in 1997. He says of his seminary experience, *God spoke to me the first day I attended classes that "education tends to pride – study hard but don't let it go to your head."*

You can learn more about Dave on his website, daveholland.org.

Dave studied the Gospel of Luke for over ten years while writing the *Daily Jesus Series*. *Every Day Jesus* is the first installment of that series. There is a brief prequel called *Christmas Jesus* that can also be ordered at DaveHolland.org. *Every Day Jesus* covers the first five chapters of Luke and the third book, *Extraordinary Jesus*, goes to print in September 2020. That book will contain the next 40 devotionals covering Luke 5b-9. Dave's plan is to continue through the books of Luke and Acts should the Lord enable him to this mission. Thanks for joining us on this journey to know Jesus *every day*.

You can learn more about Dave and his books by going to Daveholland.org. By joining the email list there you will also benefit from his blog and free postings.